8 IS ENOUGH

8 IS ENOUGH

A True Story of Life, Death, Faith, Hope…+ Love

Shannon Alford

CREATION
HOUSE

8 Is Enough by Shannon Alford
Published by Creation House
A Charisma Media Company
600 Rinehart Road
Lake Mary, Florida 32746
www.charismamedia.com

Design Director: Bill Johnson
Cover design by Terry Clifton

Visit the author's website: www.247worshipministries.com

Library of Congress Control Number: 2012948816
International Standard Book Number: 978-1-62136-322-4
E-book International Standard Book Number: 978-1-62136-323-1

First edition

12 13 14 15 16 — 987654321
Printed in the United States of America

DEDICATION

This book is dedicated to my brother, Michael, and my sister-in-law, Stacey, who loved their six children and each other. Although they went to be with the Lord earlier than expected, they are now reunited with their son, Daniel, who died from a heart defect. I know they are glad to see him and will be equally excited to have all their children together again someday. We love and miss you both!

ACKNOWLEDGMENTS

I WOULD LIKE TO thank many people who loved and supported me through this project.

Sion, you are a wonderful husband, father, and best friend. You are an absolute gift from God. I thank Him every day for you and the pillar of strength you are to this family.

Mom, you have always been there for me, and I'm the mother I am today because of you.

Jerry, thank you for taking care of Mom and treating her like a queen.

Dad, you have blessed me by loving these children and encouraging all of us to work hard and be diligent.

Cindy, thank you for allowing Dad to visit us. It means so much to me.

Mimi Robson, you are the most beautiful grandmother inside and out. We love and appreciate you!

Thank you, Stacie Jennings (Vision Communications), for forming a timeline that allowed me to share my heart and the message of this story.

Thank you, Pastor Robert, Debbie, and Gateway Church, for loving and blessing us as a family.

Thank you, *8 Is Enough* group. You are wonderful "little" people, and I love you very much.

CONTENTS

FOREWORD

Through the course of life, each of us goes through seasons of pain, heartache, and loss. In our hearts, we know God didn't create a world full of war, injustice, violence, or sickness. But because Satan introduced sin into this world, those things entered our world, and we have to now live in a fallen world and endure suffering.

We have hope, though, because Jesus personally knows what it's like to live in this fallen world. He knows what it's like to lose a friend, to lose a family member. He became a human like us, and He truly understands our pain and suffering. Through all of our grief and heartache, He is right there with us, leading us through storms and working beauty out of ashes.

In *8 Is Enough*, you'll read one such story of how God is always present in the midst of our pain. Shannon and the Alford family experienced devastating loss and difficult challenges, yet through it all, you can see God's divine hand behind the scenes, creating life out of death.

Overnight, the lives of the Alford family flipped upside down. And during the past few years, we have personally witnessed Shannon, Sion, and their children work through the difficult process of combining two families into one in the midst of total upheaval. But what is truly remarkable to us is the genuine joy which Shannon and her family have exhibited and continue to demonstrate each and every day. Their testimony is truly one of God's faithfulness in every situation.

As you read Shannon's story, we encourage you to spend some time asking God what He wants to reveal to you through these pages. Ask Him to open your eyes to the hurts and needs of those around you. And then ask Him to show you how you can tangibly demonstrate His love to those experiencing pain in their lives.

—Pastors Robert and Debbie Morris
Gateway Church, Dallas/Fort Worth, Texas
Co-authors, *The Blessed Marriage*

INTRODUCTION

Living Worship

Therefore, I urge you, brothers, in view of God's mercy, to offer your bodies as living sacrifices, holy and pleasing to God—this is your spiritual act of worship. Do not conform any longer to the pattern of this world, but be transformed by the renewing of your mind. Then you will be able to test and approve what God's will is—his good, pleasing and perfect will.

—ROMANS 12:1–2

NO MATTER WHO you are, your life is worship. Worship is not something you go and do but something you live. As we live, we all long to know what we are created to do. In this passage the apostle Paul gives us three steps to knowing God's good, acceptable, and perfect will for our lives.

First, give your life to Him daily as a sacrifice. In other words, develop a prayer life so that you give Him your life daily and ask for help to live like Him. Second, give up your natural, carnal nature that is like the world. O God, how we need Your grace! (Grace is the supernatural power that enables you to do what truth demands.) Finally, give in to allowing Him to change you by daily washing yourself with the Word of God. It's the truth you know that sets you free (John 8:32).

My seventeen-year-old son, Si Alford, wrote it this way:

> I have often heard it said that life is worthless without a bank account with seven digits or that the party scene is where you will find fulfillment. Some would even say it's a matter of perspective—how you perceive everything around you and that really everyone is happy because they are doing what they want to do. I beg to differ. Life, simply put, is only fulfilling through a relationship with Christ. Nothing else will fill the gap that aches inside and begs to be filled with life.
>
> I walk through high school and see hurting, broken people who daily put themselves through the same routine, and I've got to tell you, it looks absolutely miserable. The people partying, doing drugs, and having sex all look completely and utterly miserable. But knowing this simple fact drives me forward, not because I am all high and mighty or know more Bible verses than them, but because the answer is right in front of them if they simply open their eyes and realize what Jesus has done for them. The sacrifice He made, if fully realized, would turn my classmates around so quickly, you would not recognize them the next day. You know why? Because that aching gap in their heart would be filled.
>
> The tragedy my family has experienced has only awakened my own eyes to this simple truth: that all around us are hurting people who are looking for a Savior, and I have the ability,

> through Christ in me, to free people from bondage and allow them to experience the same life and freedom that engulfs every aspect of my life.
>
> So when reading this book, don't look at it as a story of some people who had some bad stuff happen and then they thanked God for how it all worked out. No! Instead, when you hear this story, open up your heart and allow God to begin to reveal people around you who are hurting and need a Savior. Whether it's in the workplace, the grocery store, or a high school, allow God to speak to you, and then simply obey and watch what God can do.
>
> Life is unexpected. Many would call this story a tragedy. Again, I beg to differ. This story is about how, through a tragedy, God worked out something far beyond what we expected or even hoped for in our lives. Let God blow your mind. Because, trust me, He will—you've just got to let Him.

We pray this book will be a blessing not only to the scattered and broken but also to those families who have much to be thankful for. In both camps God is faithful, so let His will be done in you and let your life become "living worship."

SINCERELY,
SHANNON, SION, ELIZABETH, SI, MARY CATHERINE,
BROOKE, EMILY, AUSTIN, DAVID, AND CAROLINE

Chapter 1

KNOW HIM

IT WAS A typical Thursday morning in May as my two boys, Si and Austin, stumbled out of bed, quickly dressed for school, and ran downstairs to fight over who would eat the last of the toasted waffles. Just as I yelled up the staircase for my daughter, Brooke, to come down and eat, the phone rang. It was only a few minutes after seven. *Who could be calling this early in the morning?*

I answered the phone and heard the anguished sound of my mom crying on the other end. I couldn't understand a word she was saying. I stepped out of the kitchen and went into my bedroom where I could calm her without alarming the children.

"Mom, take a deep breath and start over," I whispered.

"Oh, Shannon," she sobbed, "Stacey had a heart attack in the middle of the night and passed away."

Immediately I fell to the floor and wept. I couldn't believe what I had just heard. All I could think about was the commitment my husband and I had made to my brother three years earlier, just before he'd died of cancer. We had promised that if anything ever happened to his wife, Stacey, we would take all five of their children.

I had three children of my own, so in my thinking, three plus five equaled *8 Is Enough.*

How could this be happening, and what was I going to do?

Why is it that life is full of situations and circumstances that cause us to stop and ask for clear direction? God never intended for us to be separated from Him. In fact, it's when we are placed in difficult situations and our backs are against the wall that we realize we need a power higher than ours to make the right decisions in life. That's when we all want a God larger, stronger, and wiser than ourselves.

My husband, Sion, was in our home office, packing his briefcase for the one-hour drive to work when I told him about the call I'd just received from my mother.

"OK, Shannon," he said as he wrapped his arms around me. "The first thing we need to do is tell the children. Then I'll call the office and let them know what happened while you call the kids' schools and get someone to take your place in the carpool this morning. We'll leave as soon as we get everything into the car."

Si, Brooke, and Austin, ages fourteen, thirteen, and ten respectively, were as stunned as I was at the news that their Aunt Stacey had died. After all, it had only been three years since they'd lost their Uncle Michael. Despite their shock and sadness, they were excited that they would soon get to be with their cousins, who ranged in age from four to fifteen.

Our family of five had converged several times each year in my hometown of Panama City, Florida, where both of my parents and my brother's family still lived. The eight cousins loved spending endless hours at the beach together, swimming in the beautiful Gulf waters, collecting shells, and building sand castles. My three children had no idea that their aunt's death meant we would all come together as one family.

The next hour was a whirlwind of activity at the Alford house as we gathered the clothing we'd need for the next week and packed our bags. I also gathered plenty of bottled water and snacks for the thirteen-hour drive from our home in Mansfield, Texas, to Panama City, Florida.

Once we pulled onto I-20 heading for Louisiana, my mind turned to the seemingly insurmountable list of things that needed to be taken care of and the decisions that had to be made. I knew my mom and dad would likely assist Stacey's mother with funeral arrangements. But how were the children going to deal with the events of the coming days?

After my brother's death, the children were devastated at losing their fun-loving father figure who had made their backyard seem like Wally World amusement park. Elizabeth, the oldest of my brother's children, was especially affected by his death because of the fond memories of her dad taking her with him to work and to run errands. Yet now, much of the responsibility of raising the children was placed heavily upon her shoulders.

Mary Catherine, the second oldest with the nickname MC given to her by her father, focused her attention on swimming competitively on a team, which pleased her mom. She coped with the grief of losing her dad by staying busy with friends.

Emily, the third child, as loving and tenderhearted as she was, had developed a bad case of middle child syndrome. Many situations left her feeling unloved and left out.

David was the only son since their brother, Daniel, had died at home ten days after his birth due to a heart defect. David was totally outnumbered by all of his sisters' estrogen-leveled chants of the motto "girls rule and boys drool." He had serious anger management issues and was often left helpless to defend himself.

Caroline, the baby of the family, was just two years old when her father passed away. She only knew him by pictures and the stories she'd heard about him from others.

All of this was racing through my mind as I thought of these five children and tried to imagine what the future looked like for them. Thankfully they had their grandparents, as well as several aunts and uncles on their mother's side of the family, who lived nearby. Yet each time I thought of seeing them face-to-face, my eyes would well up with tears.

It was then that I realized Sion and I would be putting into practice the years of teaching and hearing about prophetic praise—you know, the kind of praise that acknowledges God for what He's going to do on the basis of what you know about Him and His Word. God comforted us by reminding us of His Word in Romans 8:28: "And we know that in all things God works for the good of those who love him, who have been called according to his purpose." And in Jeremiah 29:11 we read, "'For I know the plans I have for you,' declares the Lord, 'plans to prosper you and not to harm you, plans to give you hope and a future.'"

Sion and I didn't want our kids to know we'd been designated as their cousins' guardians, because we didn't want to give them any false expectation. Worse yet, we certainly didn't want them saying, "Guess what? You're going to come live with us." So we looked for opportunities to whisper under our breath as we drove, sharing various scenarios of possible logistics while Si, Brooke, and Austin were busy with music and games or napping.

After sixteen years of marriage Sion understood that I process information verbally, meaning I like to vocalize ideas and scenarios. I appreciated the fact that as Sion drove, he was allowing me to deal with what we were facing in my own way. I also appreciated the fact that once we had all of the information regarding Michael and Stacey's wishes, including their will, he would become engaged and put his leadership skills to work.

As an executive pastor of one of the largest churches in the Dallas-Fort Worth metroplex, Sion had oversight of scheduling and managing worship teams and musicians for more than thirty weekly events held at each of the church's two area campuses. He had become an amazing budget-crunching administrator to a rapidly growing church body. This kind of leadership skill is not something that is acquired. One is born with it, and I love and appreciate this quality about him.

As we drove, I tried to wrap my head around the idea of how making the transition to a new life was going to work for all of us. Stacey's kids would be out of school for summer break in just a week, but my kids still had three weeks of school remaining. At first we'd considered having Sion take our children back to Texas while I stayed in Florida to take care of my four nieces and one nephew, but since Sion had to drive one hour each way to and from work every day, we realized this was not a good plan. Besides, our children needed me at home to help them finish the school year.

All of this was going through my mind, and at the same time I was crying and wondering how Michael and Stacey's kids were going to handle this terrible loss after all they'd already been through. David had stayed with us the previous summer, and I knew he already had a great deal of anger and frustration stemming from his father's death. I wondered how he was going to process the loss of his mother. And then there were the potential group rivalries that could happen as a result of living under one roof—like five girls sharing the same bathroom.

At that point I began looking forward to a good night's sleep.

We pulled into a gas station just outside of Panama City a few minutes after midnight. The kids were fast asleep, so I got out of the car and stood next to Sion while he pumped gas. Just as it occurred to me that I must be quite a sight after being in the car for thirteen tearful hours, Sion leaned over and kissed me.

"Happy anniversary," he said with a smile.

Happy anniversary? What is he talking about? Then I realized it was now May 15, our seventeenth wedding anniversary.

"Happy anniversary to you too," I said as I slipped my arms around his neck. Then I asked him, "Would you have married me if I'd told you we were going to be raising eight children?"

"No," he said with as straight a face as I'd ever seen.

That's when we both burst out laughing. We really needed the comic relief, because at that point the reality of what was about to happen was beginning to set in. Our family was never going to be the same. *Could we face the challenge of never again being just five, but now ten?*

When we returned to the car for the short drive to my mother's house, I leaned my seat back, closed my eyes, and thought about the wonderful man who was seated next to me: my husband and the father of my children.

I first met Sion Augustus Alford IV during my junior year of high school. He was a young, tall, dark, and handsome pre-pharmacy student at Chipola Junior College with an offer to attend the University of Florida, home of the Gators, the following year. Sion played the piano for my local church youth group on Saturday nights. He was from Chipley, Florida, a small town fifty miles north of my hometown of Panama City.

One night, after talking with him for more than an hour after the youth fellowship, I went home and told my parents all about this wonderful young man. The first thing my mom asked was if he was an American. After all, the name Sion (pronounced like the biblical name Zion, only with an S) was pretty unusual for our native Redneck Riviera.

"Yes, Mom, he's an American," I replied. "He invited me to go water skiing this coming Tuesday, and he wants to come by the house and pick me up at noon."

My dad patted me on the back and said, "That's good, Shannon," and continued watching the news. "OK," Mom said as she turned to look at me in the eyes and recite the conditions. "Bring him by the office as soon as he picks you up so we can meet him before he takes you off water skiing to a lake we've never seen."

My parents, Sam and Jeanne Schwartz, had worked hard at building their dental practice. As the office manager, Mom was in charge of hiring and payroll. All the employees loved her funny personality and generous heart. If anyone had a problem or needed someone to talk to, Mom's office provided a safe haven to run to for advice.

As she saw us coming up the back walkway the following Tuesday, she came out of her office to meet Sion. I could tell at once by her facial expressions that she liked him. She invited us in and then went to see if Dad could join us for a few minutes between taking care of his patients.

Both of my parents were fun and friendly people, and Sion didn't seem nervous at all. I got their blessing, and off we went to Crystal Lake. I learned later that my mom had at first been skeptical of a young college kid wanting to take her high school daughter to the lake. But she told me later that as soon as she met him, the Lord spoke to her and said, "Look, Nathanael [a disciple of Jesus], in whom there is no guile."

At that time I attended a small Christian school. My parents had selected it because it sheltered me from the pressures of larger schools and gave me the opportunity to learn more about the Bible. I decided not to cheer my senior year so that I could be more involved with the youth group and be with Sion as much as possible. I'd grown up singing, yet I'd always felt like I was a dime-a-dozen singer. But our youth pastor believed in mentoring young people, and he allowed Sion and me to be leaders among our peers. He gave us the opportunity every Saturday night to sing in the band, minister, and experience the presence of God firsthand. Through that youth group God birthed in us a passion for ministry. Sion would later joke that he'd crammed two years of junior college into three during those years, but God had planned for our paths to cross—and I'm so glad they did.

Sion and I dated throughout our college years, despite the fact that we attended rival schools. He attended the University of Florida in Gainesville, and I studied at Florida State University in Tallahassee. We both graduated in May of 1992, me with a bachelor's degree in fashion merchandising and marketing, and Sion with his doctorate in pharmacy. (We've since made it a tradition to sit at opposite ends of the couch when the two teams play football right after Thanksgiving every year.) Two weeks after graduation we were married in a beautiful ceremony, surrounded by beloved members of the Schwartz and Alford families and many of our friends.

A month prior to our marriage, Sion had visited his sister and her husband in Columbus, Ohio, where they attended a church that had a Bible school for worship leaders. This visit stirred up a word that had been spoken over him and his gift before we met. A former Integrity music worship leader had declared Sion would write music that would go all over the world. We had always talked about finding a place where we could serve and be involved in worship, and we felt that this church was where God wanted us to begin.

Before we could move to Ohio, Sion had to take the Florida boards in order to obtain his pharmacist license. He passed the Florida exam, and then he went on to pass the Ohio exam as well. Soon afterward he was hired at a

Kroger pharmacy in Ohio, and we moved in June of 1992 to the town of Pickerington, right outside Columbus.

Both Sion and I had been raised in the warm climate of the South. Although we were not all that excited about the cold northern weather, as newlyweds we were totally excited about the new adventure that lay before us. I have to admit Dad was right when he described Ohio's weather as arctic cold. To cope with the freezing winter temperatures, I would take a shower twice a day just to knock off the chill. We definitely were not accustomed to gray skies and not seeing the sun for months, but Sion and I loved the Bible school and we loved our church.

Because I needed to be available for our weekday morning Bible classes and on weekends for services, I couldn't work a regular retail job. However, on the first Sunday service we attended, I read in the bulletin that the church's Christian academy needed a family living and home economics teacher. I applied for the job and was hired; God's plan was coming together perfectly. We could go to Bible school five days a week in the morning and then pack our lunch and go to work in the afternoons. Sometimes Sion worked late into the evenings in addition to long hourly shifts on Friday and Saturdays every other weekend. But we were young and excited to be a part of such a dynamic ministry, so we just made it happen. What an exciting place to be! We volunteered in the music department and either sang in the choir or on the worship team every time the doors were open.

As a newlywed, there were times I wished we weren't spending so much time at church. But I thought the more I did for God, the more He would love me and we would live happily ever after. With this quest in mind, we both worked hard to prove our love and devotion to the church and to God. We were very zealous and passionate about being a part of the church and developing relationships with people who were already doing what we wanted to do.

Attending the worship school was amazing for Sion and me. We loved the anointed teaching we received from the worship leader, and it wasn't long before he and his wife became close friends. We were inspired as we watched them write songs and then go on to record albums that were distributed nationally.

When this amazing couple felt the call to move to Orlando to start a church the following year, they asked us to consider joining them to help with administration and sing with the team. The year we spent in Ohio attending the worship school had given us a firm foundation in our calling. Now we were about to step out and put that education to use. Besides, Orlando was only six hours away from home. Our families were excited for us to be moving close enough to see them on a regular basis.

I got a job as a fourth grade teacher at a Christian school, and Sion worked at a local Eckerd pharmacy while we served faithfully at the church and helped it grow. We led worship for the youth, and we were also on the Sunday morning worship team. We were walking in our calling and growing in our understanding of praise and worship, but God was drawing us to know Him more.

One of the apostle Paul's greatest prayers for us is found in Ephesians 1:17. It says, "I keep asking that the God of our Lord Jesus Christ, the glorious Father, may give you the Spirit of wisdom and revelation, so that you may know him better." One day God revealed this scripture to Sion in prayer. And with that, Sion and I began to pray for wisdom and revelation over our lives so that we could know Him more. When we were dating, we would pray and tell God we were giving Him our lives and would do whatever He wanted to do through us. Little did we know that God was now setting us up for another transition and move.

We received a call from our hometown church with an offer to return to Panama City to serve as both the youth pastors and the praise and worship leaders. Sion and I were thrilled because we had discovered that I was pregnant and would become parents sometime in November. While we enjoyed being only six hours away from our families, we now longed to be even closer. We were more than ready to go home and be reunited with friends and family, especially since my brother Michael and his wife, Stacey, were expecting their first child at any moment. Their daughter Elizabeth was born just two weeks before we returned to Panama City.

Sion worked at the church Monday through Thursday, and he pulled a thirteen-hour shift every Friday at Eckerd to keep up with his license and help pay the bills. I worked at my dad's office in accounts receivable Monday through Thursday and sang on the worship team every Sunday while we awaited the arrival of our son.

Sion Augustus Alford V, was born November 23, 1994, the day before Thanksgiving. Sion's mom came and stayed with us for a week to help with the cooking and laundry, and both she and my mom were instrumental in teaching me the ins and outs of caring for a newborn. I rested for two weeks and then returned to church to practice for the special Christmas program.

Sion had written a Christmas musical entitled *The Shepherd and the King*, in which I was scheduled to sing the title cut song for the presentation at the church in just three weeks. My dad played one of the wise men in the musical, and he was going to lift baby Si up as Mufasa lifted Simba in *The Lion King*. Si made it to some of his first debut performances, but not all of them. When he was at the church, a friend of mine stayed with him in an off-stage room, and I ran back and forth to nurse him between scenes.

I didn't want to slow down and not be a part of everything, but I see now that I placed my performance and my desires before his needs. Little Si was only three weeks old, and I was pushing him to the limits to be a star. Sometimes wisdom comes with age, and I now realize how selfish I was for pushing him. What he really needed was his mom and his own bed, but we were caught up fulfilling the prophetic promise instead of living in God's will for our lives.

For the next two years my parents enjoyed watching their family grow as my sister-in-law, Stacey, and I presented them with grandchildren on a regular basis. After the birth of our daughter, Brooke, in 1996 and our second son, Austin, in 1998, Sion and I decided our family of five was complete. I was totally outnumbered with Si being three and Brooke being two years old when Austin was born. My friends would ask me, "Don't you want to keep the pattern going: boy, girl, boy, girl?" Yet both Sion and I felt a peace about our trinity. I'm so glad we did, because Michael and Stacey stayed in the race and went on to have two more children, for a total of four girls and one boy.

Not only were the 1990s a season of growth for our family, but they also marked a period of growth in ministry for Sion and me. Our pastor had a vision to reach as many people as possible, and Sion played a particularly significant part in accomplishing this goal. In addition to helping establish the church's radio and television ministries, he was also producing live musical presentations that drew people from Florida, Georgia, and Alabama. We were delighted to watch our church's congregation grow from 150 people to over 800 in what seemed like no time at all.

Sion and I were happily consumed with recording songs that were being written at the church, and we were thrilled when we released our first nationally known album, *Fresh Fire*. It was one of five albums we recorded during that period of time.

One of our favorite ministry events was the annual worship conference we conducted at our church each summer. We met so many wonderful pastors and worship leaders from all over the southeast United States, and we were especially thrilled that we could introduce them to our music. One particular couple we developed a relationship with were the worship pastors at a church in North Carolina. When they were promoted to an associate pastor position, we were offered the position of worship pastors at their church.

Initially it seemed wrong to think about leaving our home church where we'd been married, our children had been baptized, and we'd been so blessed. But we'd been there for over nine wonderful years, and for quite some time Sion and I had felt that God had something more for us. Perhaps this was His invitation for us to step out into that something more.

There are those who believe that being in ministry somehow insulates people from life's difficulties and disappointments. This is not true. While Sion and I continued to grow in the Lord and in the ministry that we were called to, we also grieved over other issues in our family.

We had watched Michael and Stacey go from social smokers to full-blown chain smokers, a condition that was now affecting their health. Both were unusually thin as a result of not eating properly, and the rest of us often expressed our concern for their health and the ultimate well-being of their children. There was so much evidence available regarding the deadly consequences of smoking, yet they were both powerless over this addictive legal narcotic.

Occasionally Sion and I would invite Michael and Stacey to come to church with us. But my brother would tell me he didn't want to play the hypocrite game, and besides, he didn't feel accepted. What a lie of the enemy! He was offended and the Bible says that a brother offended is harder to win than a walled city (Prov. 18:19).

Even more heartbreaking than my brother and sister-in-law's situation was what was going on with my parents. They'd had their ups and downs over the years as all couples do, but they were always able to make adjustments and move past their difficulties. However, since Michael and I were grown and had families of our own, the breach between my parents had grown even deeper and wider. When the decision was made to divorce, it shook our whole family.

In an effort to survive, I had formed walls to protect myself from being burdened by my family's problems. For years I had prayed for my family, desiring for them to be in ministry with me, but I was greatly disappointed. Spending time together oftentimes became strained because it seemed we were going in opposite directions.

So Sion and I saw the offer to go to North Carolina not only as the next step in God's plan for our lives but also as a way to separate ourselves from the pain of having to deal with family issues. In all our efforts to know God, we were blinded by pride, and our prayers were hindered. I couldn't see past my own hurt and pain, so I wasn't willing to lay down my life for anyone else. Isn't laying down our lives the very foundation of our Christian faith? I had to ask myself the question: Did I really know Him? While we were busy singing about revival, my family was falling apart. So you tell me what's worse, the sinner in need of a Savior or the saint who is too selfish to serve?

But aren't you glad God never gives up and was willing to lay down His life? God wants us to *know Him*.

Chapter 2

SERVE HIM

During our lifetime, each of us will experience a variety of transitions as we move from one season of life to another, so it's important to enjoy the journey and serve where God has us planted.

One of the things I love most about God is that He never allows anything in our lives without a purpose, and that purpose is always to make us more Christlike. He is continually revealing His Word to us line upon line and precept upon precept so that we are then able to step out in faith and move in the new direction He is calling us. Little did Sion and I know that we were about to step into a season of change that would last nearly three years.

Sion particularly loves growth and the aspect of moving forward on a continual basis. I, on the other hand, like to move slowly and ask a million questions. We both felt like God had prepared us to be part of something new. In fact, when we would talk about the "new something," our zeal for God would lead us to declare that we were going to do something that had never been done before. While we were busy making plans to do something new, God was working on making us new from the inside out.

After my parents divorced, my dad and I had a very strained relationship. Before knowing all of their marital problems, I always loved and honored my dad. In fact, I would sing a song about him: "Anything your dad can do, my dad can do better." I came out of the womb that way. The entire family loved and clambered after his attention.

Although it was hard to say good-bye to our family, our church, and our pastor who had been such an integral part of our life and ministry for so many years, we knew it was time to move forward. My parents had both remarried and moved on in their new lives, so Sion and I were ready for a new change as well.

Our first stop during our season of transition was in Fayetteville, North Carolina, where we labored for nine months with the amazing couple we'd met through our worship conferences. This couple was so gracious to us throughout our time with them. They appreciated the fact that we'd moved our family ten hours away from home and put our children in new schools.

In addition to serving as an assistant worship pastor, Sion used the expertise he'd gained at our home church to assist in the building of a studio at the Fayetteville church. Because of the connections we'd developed through the worship conferences in Panama City, we oftentimes received invitations to come to a church and hold a conference.

I accompanied Sion as often as I could at the conferences, where we would usually begin with a "Night of Worship," followed by a day of instruction. I worked with the choir and taught two classes, one on learning the vocal parts and practical issues, and the other on a worshipper's heart. Sion worked with the worship teams, teaching about the difference between praise and worship and on why worship leaders do what we do. I wasn't able to participate in these conferences as consistently as when I had my family nearby to look after the children, yet the ministry continued to grow and flourish.

Sion and I remained sensitive to the fact that we were in a season of transition. The time came when we both felt we'd completed our assignment in Fayetteville, but we had no direction about moving forward. The Bible says that "a man's heart plans his way, but the LORD directs his steps" (Prov. 16:9, NKJV), so we decided we would just enjoy Christmas with our family in Panama City and let the Lord take care of directing our steps. Of course, our decision didn't stop us from reminding Him that we'd leaped out in faith and had trusted Him for direction.

On the drive home to Panama City that December, we received a call from a friend of ours telling us about a growing church in Arlington, Texas, that was looking for a worship leader. They wanted someone who would be a part of the church on a consistent basis and who could help them pastor a choir. Our friend asked if we'd be interested, and we said yes.

My mom agreed to keep the children for a few days while we flew to Texas to meet with the couple who served as pastors of the church. They'd been holding services in a local high school while renovation on the building they had purchased was being completed. When we found out the church had an academy that our children could attend, Sion and I knew this was where God wanted us to be. We accepted the invitation to join the staff, and for the next two years we served as worship pastors for the church while Si, Brooke, and Austin attended the elementary school academy.

While we loved being part of the church, we were

anxiously awaiting the opportunity to begin recording our own worship albums again. Sion and I would stay up late talking about evangelistic ways to reach more people, and the time came when once again we felt it was time to step out.

We formally established our ministry and gave it the name of "24/7 Worship Ministries." Working with a database of names we'd collected since we first began conducting our worship conferences in Panama City, we quickly developed a group of monthly partners who faithfully supported the ministry. Oftentimes a group of several small churches would come together at one location where Sion would present a two-day seminar teaching worship leaders about intimacy with God through worship. I wasn't able to travel with him because of the children, but at least we were writing and recording our own songs again.

In 2006 we were invited to attend a worship leadership luncheon being held at Gateway Church in Southlake, Texas, about an hour from our home. Worship leaders from all over the Dallas-Fort Worth metroplex gathered in order to glean from each other, and Sion and I were thrilled to be a part of the event. That day we received a book entitled *From Dream to Destiny: The Ten Tests You Must Go Through to Fulfill God's Purpose for Your Life*. The book, which was written by Gateway's pastor, Robert Morris, really ministered to Sion and me in our time of transition.

Although there were times when money was tight, reading Pastor Robert's book gave us the peace that came from knowing God knew right where we were. What He was doing in us would prepare us for what we would be doing in the future. It is through the tests and pits of life that we learn the journey is truly our reward.

Sion and I were not the only ones in our family who were going through a transition. Michael and Stacey had come to realize that hanging out with a company of friends who were smoking and drinking was not benefiting them or their family. Michael in particular had reached the point where he understood that he was going down the wrong road.

They became acquainted with several families who attended a vibrant Methodist church in Panama City, and it wasn't long before Michael, Stacey, and the kids were attending as well. The children got involved in the youth ministry, and Michael and Stacey became active in the children's ministry, helping in the nursery as any good member would do. Michael was always what I'd describe as a people person, meaning he had lots of friends whom he loved to help anytime there was a need. I'd always believed that he was an evangelist at heart, and my prayer was that we'd one day be in ministry together. For now I was just happy to see them all involved at their church.

Since my parents' divorce, our trips home to Panama City two or three times each year had not been as joyful as they'd once been. A subtle sense of tension always seemed to hang over our heads as we tried to keep things as normal as possible for the kids while scheduling separate visiting times with each of their grandparents. Yet despite the adjustments our family was making, when it was time to go home for Thanksgiving, I was especially excited about getting to spend time with my brother and his family, now that they were headed in a new direction.

My mom always loved having all of her grandchildren gathered together at Thanksgiving, and that year was no exception. The aroma of the baking turkey filled the house, and since it would still be several hours before dinner was ready, we all decided to go outside and play a game of football. Sion and Michael were warming up, tossing the ball back and forth to each other. That's when I noticed that Michael's throw looked peculiar; he was just side-arming the ball instead of really throwing it as he normally did. Sion teased him, saying, "Come on, man, throw the ball right," and the kids joined in with, "Uncle Michael, throw the ball! Throw the ball!"

Michael explained that he'd been having what he thought was an issue with his rotator cuff, probably a result of the construction job he was working on. When we brought up his inability to throw the football again at dinner, my mom told him he really needed to go see a doctor.

"OK, Mom," he said with a wink in my direction, "I'll make an appointment right after the holidays." I knew my brother well enough to know he'd find a way to just push through the pain and wait for the arm to heal itself.

Just as I'd suspected, Michael didn't go to the doctor after Thanksgiving, nor did he go to the doctor after Christmas. In January he finally saw a doctor. When the X-rays didn't show anything unusual, the doctor agreed that it must be his rotator cuff and said it would just take some time to heal. But then in March of 2006, he went to the doctor again after discovering a growth in the area of his neck and shoulder. At the same time his face began to droop. An MRI was scheduled on the morning of March 10, which was his daughter Emily's birthday.

My mom accompanied Michael and Stacey to the appointment, and it was there that the doctor informed them my brother had lung cancer. The doctor said the visible growth, known as a pan-coast tumor, had formed from the cancer in Michael's lungs. The tumor was also causing his face to droop. A follow-up appointment was scheduled to discuss a treatment plan.

Afterward, as they walked in stunned silence to the car, my mom asked Michael, "What are you going to do?"

"I'm going to go celebrate my daughter's birthday," he said.

Sion and I arrived with our three children the following week for spring break. Instead of all of us staying together at a family beach house as planned, Michael and Stacey left the children with us so that they could focus on the issue at hand. Mom joined us at the beach house to be with all of her grandchildren, and I loaded up the van with the kids anytime we went to visit my dad.

Though everyone was having a great time during our stay, we were concerned for Michael. My parents individually assisted him and Stacey in setting medical appointments while Sion and I kept the kids occupied. At that point Michael's kids knew their dad was sick; they just didn't know the extent of the situation. We all tried to stay positive for the kids, but we knew Michael would be facing a difficult journey that would begin with possible surgery, followed by months of chemotherapy.

While our fractured family was preparing to fight the good fight of faith, Michael and Stacey were also making preparation for their children's future. My mother told me that they'd gone to see an attorney for the purpose of writing a will, and they wanted to come and talk to Sion and me about it.

"One of the questions they have to answer is about the children," she said. "They need to establish a guardian for them, should the need arise, and they want to ask you if you and Sion would be willing to accept that responsibility. I just want to give you and Sion some time to think about it before they arrive."

Later that afternoon the mood was serious as Mom, Michael, Stacey, Sion, and I sat down together. I can only imagine how difficult it was for my brother to ask, "If anything were ever to happen to Stacey, would you be willing to take all five of the kids?"

Before we could answer, Stacey added, "We wouldn't want them to be split up; we'd want them to stay together so they could draw strength from each other."

The possibility of neither Michael nor Stacey being able to raise their children was something I just couldn't wrap my head around. But Sion and I talked about all of the "what-ifs" where their children were concerned, and we affirmed that we would always do anything we could for them.

When Michael and Stacey said good-bye to us at the end of the week, they had the assurance that we would indeed be there for their children—all of them—should that time ever come.

Shortly after we returned to Texas, my mom, Michael, and Stacey had a final meeting with the attorney who was drawing up their will. When they got to the part that addressed the children, Michael and Stacey told him that Sion and I were their first choice of designated guardians, followed by Stacey's brother and his wife, who lived in South Florida.

"Let me ask you this," the attorney said. "If either of these couples is unable to take all five of the children, are you willing to have them split up?"

"Absolutely not," Stacey said. "I want all of them to be together."

Turning to Michael, he asked, "Are you sure your sister and her husband are willing to do this?"

"Yes, I am," Michael said. "Mom was there when we talked to Shannon and Sion about the will, and they know they are going to be named the designated guardians."

"All right then. I'll draw up the document and will let you know when it's ready for your signatures."

My mom and I talked on a regular basis, and she kept me up-to-date on Michael's chemotherapy. My dad usually spent the night in the hospital room with him, and Mom and Stacey took turns being with him during the day. No one wanted him to be left alone during this grueling process. His cancer was growing rapidly, and by the first of May it had already metastasized from his lungs to his bones. This was not good news. He was trying to function as normally as possible and be there for the kids, who were now dealing with the reality of their father's illness.

The chemotherapy was particularly difficult for Michael. In the past there had been times when he'd drink a couple of beers and smoke cigarettes all day long without actually eating any food. With no nutrients to keep his body going, the effects of the chemotherapy were devastating. He lost all of his beautiful, thick, curly brown hair, plus he had boils on his forehead from all the medications.

Michael was on morphine to help manage the pain, but he didn't like being on the drug because he felt like he was not alert enough to respond to anyone. To help relieve the pain, in his living room he built a harness that was used to elevate his arms. His body ached to the point that he would often ask the older girls to rub his shoulders and neck as hard as they could.

During this time an incident occurred that the children still retell today as if it had happened only yesterday. Michael had built a bookshelf for their living room but had not yet securely attached it to the wall. It was decorated with books, pictures, and other items that were all too tempting for little Caroline. She decided life was too boring and began to climb up to reach for a movie on one of the shelves.

Stacey and their oldest daughter, Elizabeth, had gone to the store. Michael was resting on the couch, and the other children where either playing or watching TV when they heard the crash and screams. Emily and David watched their dad move faster than they had ever seen, and they witnessed him grimace with pain as he single-handedly lifted the bookshelf off their baby sister. As Michael picked up a frightened Caroline from the rubble and wiped the tears from her cheeks, they all gathered around her, amazed that she had no apparent bumps or bruises from the incident. Even today Caroline proudly tells the story of her heroic daddy saving her life since she's heard it so many times from her older siblings.

Despite Michael's situation and physical ailments, he

managed to keep going to church. He would sit on the back row or in a designated room for nursing mothers when it was unoccupied, because it was too painful to sit for any length of time in the same place. Michael wanted God to heal him. He would stay up late reading his Bible and sharing with Mom and his family what God had showed him in his quiet times. But by then it was determined that the cancer was stage four, and the doctors said they'd done all they could do. His lifespan was short.

We were all in denial at the time. We were praying and believing that God would turn the situation around as Michael went through his next round of chemo, but his body was just too weak to go through it. We continued to believe for a miracle, that against all odds he would recover.

Everyone who loved Michael wanted to do what they could to help him. In times of illness there is great stress as each person seeks to do the right thing, though they may not agree on what the right thing is. This was true in our family as everyone sought to do what they felt was best. It was a difficult time for the children, especially the older ones who witnessed the disagreements over what was best for their dad.

My brother's illness was not the only issue we were dealing with at that time. Sion's mother, herself a cancer survivor and known as a miracle child at MD Anderson in Houston, Texas, had come to the place where she needed the kind of care that Sion's dad could not give her. The decision was made that they would move from Florida to Colorado, where Sion's sisters could assist their parents. Sion and I agreed to help his dad close down the house and move, so our family was off to Florida again the first week of June. I was glad that we were going, because I desperately wanted to see my brother, and I would've done anything for Mrs. Alford.

Since the day I'd first met her, she loved me and treated me as if I were her own. She was a retired kindergarten teacher with a heart of gold, and all of the children loved going to Mimi Alford's house. We all marveled at her patient teaching skills and praised her for the generous, loving ways she showed all of her grandchildren. We had spent many fun-filled holidays in the heartwarming old Alford estate, where Mrs. Alford loved cooking and decorating for special family occasions.

Although it was hard to believe those special times had come to an end, none of us thought twice of giving back to her all that she had given to us. She had been a prayer warrior and had served all of us, and now she needed us to serve her.

Looking back, I can see that it was her example of "living worship" that made it easy for us to follow and serve. The Bible says, "The Son of Man did not come to be served, but to serve, and to give his life as a ransom for many" (Matt. 20:28). When we are willing to serve Him and lay down our lives for someone else, God can change a selfish heart that wants to be served into one that is open and willing to serve.

For two weeks I worked with Sion during the day as we helped his dad decide what furniture would be taken to Colorado, which items would be given to Sion and his sisters, and what would be sold at a garage sale. During the day I packed boxes and cleaned, and at night I drove to Panama City to see Michael.

It was painful for me to see my brother in what we

knew were the final stages of his life. Each time I saw him and witnessed Stacey and the children's struggles, all I could do was sob. I was of little comfort to them. Each night when I returned to Chipley to be with Sion, I was exhausted from the grief I was experiencing over what was happening. But then one day, in the midst of all of the family turmoil, it was as if God hit the pause button and brought a beautiful glimmer of joy into my life.

We had promised the kids when we left North Carolina that once we moved to Texas and were settled, we'd get a dog. We'd been there for two years, but it just hadn't happened yet. My mother's husband's daughter, Renee, who lived there in Florida, raised Maltese dogs. She had one puppy from a recent litter that she couldn't sell because he was the runt. When Renee told my mom that she was looking for a home for the puppy, Mom said, "I know just the right family. Shannon would love the dog, the kids want a dog, and this cute little ball of white fur would be perfect for them."

Mom and I arranged a visit to Renee's house one afternoon to let the kids play with the puppy. They absolutely fell in love with the little guy, and I had to admit he was pretty cute as he jumped and tumbled between Si, Brooke, and Austin. That's when Renee said to them, "Would you like to keep him?"

"Yes, yes, yes," they all yelled. Then they looked at me and said, "Please, Mom, can we keep him? Can we?" followed by their promises to take care of him, potty train him, and teach him tricks.

"You can keep him," I said. Of course, I was thinking, "OK, this is going to be like having another kid. All we need is a little time to get into a routine and then everything will be fine."

The kids named their new puppy Dallas. The first few nights he was with us, I literally had to sleep in a separate room with him. I was up and down with him each night and then would work at the house the next day and go see my brother in the evening. It was an amazing and crazy time. Dallas and I quickly bonded, and I felt as if I were a little girl again playing with the dog I'd had throughout my years in school. Dallas brought me a sense of peace and comfort during those difficult days.

Michael was slipping away fast, and the tension between my parents and my sister-in-law over what to do about it was at an all-time high. We had now been in Florida for two weeks, and the mounting bills and other responsibilities brought Sion and me to the conclusion that it was time for us to return to Texas.

On the morning of June 13, the kids and I put Dallas in the car and began the thirteen-hour drive home so that my son Si could attend his scheduled baseball practice. Sion and his dad would leave the following day, driving a U-Haul truck filled with the items for our home and those that were going on to Colorado.

Traveling with three kids and a three-month-old puppy was a learning experience. Dallas had several puppy accidents before we figured out how to recognize the signs that he needed to do his business. But we were quick learners, and the trip went well overall.

The evening I arrived at home, I got a call from my mother informing me that Michael's condition had taken a drastic turn for the worse. "Shannon, Michael's not going to make it," she said. "We've called in hospice."

When I'd last seen him two nights earlier, he was weak but still able to get up and around. Mom said now he couldn't even get out of the hospital bed that had been brought into their home.

I felt so helpless and alone. I was more than eight hundred miles from my brother and my parents, and Sion wouldn't be home until late the following night. Knowing there was absolutely nothing I could do to help my brother, I began to sing songs of praise as I dove into the familiar routine of doing laundry and caring for my children and, of course, our new puppy.

At eight o'clock the next morning, my mother called. I didn't want to hear any more bad news, but she told me that Michael had passed away early that morning. I couldn't believe what I was hearing. I felt a cold emptiness on the inside as I slid down the side of my bed onto the floor. I felt so bad that I'd not been there with him. I also felt bad that I wasn't there for my parents, who were now grieving the loss of their son. I felt even worse for Stacey and the children, who had lost their husband and father. Michael wouldn't be there to watch his children grow, to walk his daughters down the aisle when they married, or to cheer for his son when he played ball. And what about Stacey? How in the world was she going to support and raise five children without her husband?

My children were still fast asleep as I hung up the phone. Alone in the bedroom with only Dallas to turn to, I picked up the wriggling puppy who was only too happy to lick away the tears that were streaming down my face. I paused to ask God why this had to happen that day, June 14, 2006. It was my birthday. What a terrible thing to remember on what was supposed to be a wonderful day. But I now see that God was preparing my heart to lay down my life and serve another. The Bible says, "Whoever finds his life will lose it, and whoever loses his life for my sake will find it" (Matt. 10:39). I was living life for me, but God showed me He wanted me to lay down my life for Him.

When Michael died, it was as if time stopped for me. I actually felt like I was numb for the next several days while Sion moved into gear and made everything happen. I remember that I looked at Michael's casket during the funeral service and couldn't believe what was happening. By the looks on my parents' faces, they couldn't believe it either.

During that funeral service I sat and listened to Mom, empowered by the grace of God, telling stories of my brother and the lives he had touched. I was crying so hard, it took every ounce of Sion's strength to keep me seated on the pew. I wanted to run to the altar, open the lid to the casket, and scream at the top of my lungs, "Michael, get up!"

My mother is an amazing woman. My sister-in-law, Stacey, thought Mom would lose her faith and be frustrated with God for not healing Michael. After all, she had never given up hope when she'd seen him dying. Instead, when Mom had just lost her only son, she went to another level in her faith in God and was able to stand that day and deliver a eulogy without shedding a tear. Mom was a picture of the strength of God's grace as she spoke words of comfort to family and friends.

We learned that, in the year prior to his death, Michael had made an amazing impact on many people. Throughout his battle with cancer he spent countless hours urging his friends from high school to give their lives to the Lord. Mom said it was the sweetest thing ever to see him pouring himself into the lives of his friends and sharing scriptures with them.

But his friends were not the only ones to benefit from Michael's faith and wisdom. Before he died, he called his children together so that he could speak a blessing over them. He told them, "I don't want you to be angry with God. God did not do this to me, and it is not His plan for my life. It was my own choices and decisions that caused this to happen."

Following the funeral the entire family went to a local restaurant. It was the first time since my parents had divorced that we were all together in one place, thus adding a sense of awkwardness to our grief. While some of the adults tried to keep the conversation light, my dad and I were having difficulty holding back the tears. I'm sure the waiter must have thought we were a bit strange, but God brought my dad and me back together that day. We all agreed that the most important thing from there on out was our relationship with each other and our family. It was the first step in letting go of the past hurts from the divorce. It was also a wake-up call. There was nothing we could do about Michael's death, but there was something we *could* do about his children's future.

The next day as Sion and I were preparing to fly back to Dallas, I kept asking God, "Why? What was the point of praying if You weren't going to heal Michael?" As I paused, God spoke to me and said, "Prayer is not for Me; it's for you, Shannon." He reminded me of Jesus before His death—how He went off to pray and told His disciples to do the same. Jesus went to the cross saying, "Thy will be done," and it was so.

Although we couldn't understand everything that had happened, God had nonetheless allowed it. My mother, Sion, and I held hands that day and prayed the Lord's Prayer, believing God knew all things and that He had promised to work all things for our good.

Although our family had had its differences in recent years, the loss of Michael had given everyone a new perspective. We recognized we were a group of parents, grandparents, aunts, and uncles who needed to unite in our commitment to help Michael's family by providing them with all the love and support they were going to need. We connected in a way that brought not only healing to everyone but also a willingness to serve and lay down our lives for the journey ahead. In other words, God wanted us to *serve Him*.

I think Michael, the evangelist, would have been pleased.

Chapter 3

SEEK HIM

Grief is not only a natural response to loss; it is also an intensely personal process that is defined by an individual's unique personality and beliefs. Following Michael's death, I tried to focus on going through the daily routine of doing everything I needed to do as a wife and mother. There were times when I'd feel the joy of knowing that my brother was with the Lord and experiencing no more pain, and then something would happen that would bring me again to tears. To say that my emotions were still a bit raw would be putting it mildly, as the employees of one local business found out.

Maltese dogs are known for their long, silky white coats, which can become matted if they are not regularly groomed. For this reason many owners choose to cut the coat in an easy-care puppy cut. This is what I decided to do with Dallas. When my daughter, Brooke, and I took him to our local PetSmart, the groomer said she might have to cut him a little shorter than usual to get the mats that had already formed. She assured us Dallas was in good hands and that we could pick him up in a few hours.

When Brooke and I returned later that afternoon to retrieve Dallas, who had been a little fluff ball when we'd left him there, so much of his hair had been cut that I didn't recognize him.

"Here's your dog," the groomer said with a smile as she tried to hand me a squirming white dog that looked nothing like Dallas.

"This is not my dog; it doesn't even look like my dog. I think you've made a mistake," I said adamantly, convinced that she was not giving me my dog back.

When we couldn't settle the matter after talking for a few more minutes, she put the dog on the floor and called the manager to come to the front of the store to help.

"Is there anything I can do for you, ma'am?" he asked in a polite and understanding tone.

"I brought my dog in and asked for a puppy cut, but this is not my dog," I explained.

Now, all the while Dallas was jumping around wanting me to pick him up, yet I remained convinced that he was not my dog. I was so convinced that Brooke, who has nerves of steel and never cries, was in tears because she believed this dog was not our Dallas.

The manager remained calm and said, "Let's just think this through. Do you see how the dog is responding to you? He can't wait for you to pick him up. Why don't you take him home and think about it, and then call me tomorrow and let me know if you still think he's not your dog."

I explained that I'd recently lost my brother and was still dealing with the grief of that loss. He was very patient and understanding, but I'm sure that all of the other people there must have been thinking, "This lady is really strange."

I apologized for creating an incident in the store, thanked the manager for his patience, and then I paid for the service and left. But I still wasn't completely convinced that the dog Brooke and I were taking home was Dallas. I called Sion on the phone and said, "I'm here to pick up Dallas, but I don't think it is Dallas that we're bringing home." Sion was aware of the process I'd been going through with the loss of my brother, and he tried to help me. He was so good at helping me connect the dots and realize that everything was going to be OK.

When Brooke and I got home and put the dog on the floor, he did everything Dallas usually did, including running around and recognizing where everything was. We all had a good laugh once I realized this was indeed Dallas, and the kids were relieved when I said he could stay. To this day Brooke still brings up that incident when we take Dallas to the groomer: "Mom, are you sure that when you get home, you're going to be OK and know it's your dog?"

Following the loss of Michael, Sion and I began to sense another transition was at hand. We had been attending Gateway Church for more than a year since we'd stepped out into full-time ministry, which had lived up to the name "24/7 Worship Ministries," and we had just completed the church membership classes. I had gone through vocal evaluations and was singing at church on weekends while Sion was away doing worship conferences.

One thing we'd come to appreciate about the Gateway Church culture was that they truly wanted to develop relationship with those who were drawn to be a part of the church. The leaders knew about our experience in worship ministry, but they were more interested in getting to know who we were as individuals rather than what we could do for them.

When new members are received into the church, it is customary for leadership to pray for each person or couple and speak a word of encouragement as the Holy Spirit leads. We had several such words spoken over us by different pastors that day, but two would be of particular significance where our future was concerned. In part, these are the words spoken over us by one of the pastors at the presbytery:

> "Sion, God's given you so much. He's given you so much and you've given back, but there's more coming, brother. There's some big stuff coming. The Lord comes to confirm to you tonight that you're special in this, you're a cut above, He's given you a lot, and you need to be confident in that. The Lord says, 'Relax, you're going to be successful; the dreams that you have *will* be fulfilled. But you must enjoy the journey. In order to lead others to enjoy it, you must enjoy it yourself. Simply abide and bear fruit. You don't have to strive for it. Relax and receive it. You're a good man, you're a good husband, you're a good father, and you're good in all those ways, in all those fundamental ways of calling in your life.'
>
> "Shannon, the Lord says, 'You are a mother indeed. You are an excellent, an extreme mom, and an extremely good mom.' The Lord wants to confirm this to you as a calling to you in your life, that the greatest thing that you will *ever do* is what you're *already doing* as a mother, that you were needed there and you were called there.

> They need you and needed you. We all need you. You're a gift, and you're gifted. You have a great gift of encouragement. As a matter of fact, you could be called a daughter of encouragement. You have these words of encouragement for everyone; you think it even if you don't say it. And the Lord comes to challenge you to say it more. They need it, we need it; we need your encouragement."

Gateway Church was five years old and growing at an exponential rate of speed. They already had two campuses in the Dallas-Fort Worth metroplex, which held multiple services on weekends and throughout the week. There was something going on at the church literally every night of the week. Worship was an integral part of each service or activity, from junior high to young couples to adults. Because of the rapid growth, the church leaders felt it was time to hire someone to coordinate the scheduling of worship teams, help develop a worship teaching curriculum, and handle the daily administrative needs it takes to run a department efficiently.

Sion's leadership and administrative skills, combined with his experience as a nationally recognized worship leader, made him a perfect fit for the job. So in the summer of 2007, he accepted the offer to become Gateway's executive worship pastor. While Sion worked to establish structure and organization within the departments, I continued singing with the worship team on the weekends. In order to become a vocal director, I was familiarizing myself with the individual parts of the music as well as the flow of each song.

We were thrilled that our entire family was now a

part of such a vital and vibrant church. Si, Brooke, and Austin were involved in the youth groups and activities, and both Sion and I were using the gifts and talents that God had given us. It had been a tumultuous three years of transition, but at last we felt as if we'd come home. Well, almost.

We were accustomed to making the one-hour drive from our home in Mansfield to the church in Southlake each weekend, but now Sion had to make the commute every day for work. We'd had our house on the market for almost a year when he joined the Gateway staff, but the reality of a falling market was rapidly pushing us against the wall.

Knowing that God had provided Sion's position at the church, we expected He would also quickly bring us a buyer for the house. But that didn't happen. We had plenty of showings, but not a single offer. We'd done everything our Realtor asked us to do, and we were praying day and night for a buyer. When our worship team gathered to share prayer requests each week, I continually asked that our house would sell, but nothing happened. After eighteen puzzling months of no offers, we decided to take the house off the market for a while so that we could return it to the market later as a new listing.

I remember praying and marching around my house as if it were Jericho, asking God to go to battle over the economic drought in the housing market and sell our home. I would often call my mom and talk to her on the phone about this concern. One night we were talking as she was munching on her favorite snack, popcorn. I said, "Mom, when is God going to sell our house?"

She paused from munching and said, "When God is finished doing what He is doing in you and Sion."

I fell back in the couch cushions and sighed, "What?"

She took a drink of water, cleared her throat and said, "Shannon, when you and Sion lay everything down at His feet and stop striving for what *you* want, but seek God for what *He* wants you to do, then you just watch. Everything else is going to fall into place."

I wrestled with this answer as I sat there nestled amongst all the pillows. That's when Mom grabbed her Bible and read me Matthew 6:33 (NAS): "But seek first His kingdom and His righteousness, and all these things will be added to you."

Both Sion and I spent most of our time concerned about our future, yet God wanted us to seek Him first. The proof of someone's passion is found in what they pursue. My passion was focused first on survival in a difficult season rather than on seeking God and feasting on His faithfulness. According to the book *Strengths Finder,* my second strength is responsibility, so I am usually a task-oriented person, like Martha. God wanted to balance me out and desired for me to be like Mary and to seek Him.

Proverbs 8:17 says, "I love those who love me, and those who seek me find me." This scripture is a promise from God, and we all know God does not break a promise. How does God know we love Him? We first have to define what love is. Love is simply laying down our lives at our own expense. What does it mean to lay down our lives? It means giving ourselves to God and seeking Him to find out what He wants to do through us.

God wants us to seek His kingdom, His Word, and

His ways. He wants us to seek Him as the sovereign ruler over all creation and all things. He wants us to wear His righteousness like a garment, revealing His character. God desires for us to seek Him, not because He's lonely or needs our approval, but because we need Him. We will wreck our lives without Him.

While Sion and I were battling to get our house sold, Stacey was struggling to adjust to her new life without Michael.

Michael and Stacey didn't have life insurance, and once they realized they needed it, they were unable to get it. Stacey received monthly income from Michael's Social Security benefits, but it wasn't anywhere near enough to support a family of six. With her youngest child, Caroline, in preschool, Stacey babysat other children at home so that she could be there for her daughter.

Stacey's mother and sisters helped with clothing for the kids, and my mom helped by preparing meals and doing some shopping for the family. Michael and Stacey's church family also helped, but after a short time it was clear that Stacey would need to return to her former profession on a full-time basis. As a young woman, she had been a dental assistant. That's actually how she and Michael first met when he was working in my dad's dental office as the administrator. One day Stacey came to the office to bring some lab work, and that's when our hygienist introduced them. They started dating, fell in love, and were married a year later.

Once Michael realized that his situation could be terminal, his focus turned to doing everything he could to make life easier for Stacey and the kids. Without life insurance to offset the mortgage on their house, he knew that the monthly payments would be more than Stacey could handle. He couldn't bear the thought of his family not only losing him but losing their home as well, so he decided to refinance the house at a lower interest rate to reduce the payments. Sadly, because of his medical condition, none of the institutions he talked to were able to make the loan.

Unbeknownst to anyone outside our immediate family, my mother stepped in to help. That's one of the things I love about her: she would give the shirt off her back for her family. Mom said, "OK, I'll be the bank. I'll loan the two of you the money, and you can make the payments to me."

At that point Mom literally owned their house, which turned out to be a good decision for Stacey and the kids. After Michael passed away, there were months when Stacey would say money was tight and Mom would allow her to postpone making her payment. Mom also offered to help her make a monthly budget, something that had come easily to my brother but was a difficult concept for Stacey. Needless to say, there were times when Stacey's money pressures put a strain on her relationship with my mother, but all in all, Mom remained understanding and supportive.

Meanwhile, back in Mansfield, our daily drive was getting old. We called the road we had to travel each day "The 360 Parking Lot." Highway 360 was the bumper-to-bumper traffic road we traveled from Mansfield to Southlake. Sion and I were still both driving hundreds of miles each week to and from the church while believing for a miracle where the sale of our home was concerned. It had been on the market an unbelievable three years, and now the housing market was beginning to plummet. We knew it was God's plan for us to be part of Gateway Church, and we knew it was His will for us to live closer to the church. What we couldn't understand was why it was taking so long to sell the house. Oftentimes when we prayed about it, the Lord would direct us to the verse of Scripture that says, "'For I know the plans I have for you,' declares the Lord, 'plans to prosper you and not to harm you, plans to give you hope and a future'" (Jer. 29:11).

We felt that part of God's plan for our future included mission work. The outreach of Gateway Church had been extended worldwide, and Sion and I were seeking the Lord about the desire God has given us to become involved in taking the gospel to other nations. When the invitation came in 2009 to join a prayer team from Gateway on a ten-day trip to Israel, we knew that was what God wanted us to do. We were to be part of a group that would meet with Christian congregations in Israel to assist them in areas of prayer, teaching, and praise and worship.

It was hard to say good-bye to our children as we left for the airport that morning in early May, but we knew they were in good hands with my mother, who'd come from Florida to stay with them. The twelve-hour flight from the United States to Tel Aviv was both physically and mentally taxing, but there's no way to describe the excitement we experienced upon first seeing the land of the Bible. We went to the Dead Sea, the Garden of Gethsemane, and other places we'd only read about until going on this trip. Because several members of the team, including Sion, had their guitars, we were able to experience praise and worship in many of these settings.

We even went to see the Wailing Wall, where we watched the Jews holding hands and offering their petitions to the Lord. The area was divided with men on the left and women and children on the right. I walked slowly through the murmuring crowd until I reached the wall, but I couldn't think of one thing to ask God. I could only thank Him for allowing me to be there and experience this ancient culture.

As we left the wall, we saw young teenage soldiers, both boys and girls, with guns strapped to their backs. I asked our leader about this group and was brought to tears at the explanation. Once a child graduates from school, he or she is required to serve in the military for two or three years before obtaining higher education. Although my son, Austin, would dress in camouflage and sleep outside every night if I let him, I would not want him to be forced to have guns strapped to his back and walk around looking for terrorists or any other potential danger. I'm glad to be an American; it is a blessing that can easily be taken for granted.

The church where we were to conduct our meetings with the local pastors was located in Jerusalem and featured a panoramic window overlooking the walls of the Old City. I'd always heard Jerusalem referred to as the city of gold, and once night fell, I learned why. With the city lights reflecting off the Jerusalem stone (the area's most available and commonly used building material), the entire city took on the appearance of glimmering gold.

Since only about half of the local pastors who were in

attendance spoke English, we worked with a translator who spoke both fluent English and Hebrew. As Sion and another worship pastor explained how praise and worship not only affects our lives but also creates a fertile atmosphere in which the Word of God can be taught, it was thrilling to hear their words being translated and spoken in the language of the Bible.

Sion and I loved being part of this work our church was doing in Israel, and we felt that God was using this experience to confirm that He was indeed preparing us for a very special mission assignment. During a time of personal devotion one morning in Israel, two particular scriptures caught my attention. Jesus said to His disciples, "The harvest is plentiful, but the workers are few. Ask the Lord of the harvest, therefore, to send out workers into his harvest field" (Luke 10:2). In the Book of John, He said, "Do you not say, 'Four months more and then the harvest'? I tell you, open your eyes and look at the fields! They are ripe for harvest" (John 4:35).

Sensing that Sion and I were about to enter another season of transition that had to do with missions, I uttered a prayer first spoken more than two thousand years ago by a young woman only a few miles from where I was praying: "Behold the handmaid of the Lord; be it unto me according to thy word" (Luke 1:38, KJV).

One evening as we were worshipping with a group of pastors and worship teams in the church overlooking the Old City, we moved from worship into a time of intercession. Unable to stand any longer in the hushed and holy presence that had come upon us, I knelt down and began to pray. "O Lord, bring us to the place where You are the most important thing in our lives. I ask You to come and uproot any selfishness in our hearts, and replace it with genuine care for one another. Enable us to link arms with each other in a way that we may fully accomplish Your will not only in our own lives but also in the lives of others."

I thought I was praying for the churches in Jerusalem, for the connections we were making, and over all of the things God was doing that week. But I'd walked with the Lord long enough to know not to limit Him with my own restricted thinking.

We'd kept in daily contact with Mom and the kids through our Internet video service, which allowed us to see them while we talked. One morning when I got my daily call from my mom, I knew the minute I saw her face that something was wrong. My aunt Linda, Mom's sister, who had been battling breast cancer for over a year had just passed away. Mom had to return to Florida, which meant that Sion and I had to leave immediately.

As Sion and I packed our bags to return to Texas, I was grieving for my mother almost as much as I was grieving for my aunt and cousins. It had only been three years since Mom had lost her son, and now she'd lost her sister in yet another untimely passing. Aunt Linda had always held a special place in my mom's heart, because Mom was the one who had led her to the Lord. She was especially dear to me because she had been my own refuge when Mom and Dad were not getting along. She was also a huge encouragement in teaching me vocal parts and voice.

I had fond memories of Mom loading Michael and

me into the car to visit Aunt Linda and our cousins. She would incorporate me into her church specials, and I would hop right up and sing the soprano harmony part whenever she and my cousin Kim were singing at their local church. Aunt Linda encouraged Kim and me to become worship leaders and be all that God had called us to be. I loved my aunt and knew she would be missed for her encouraging words and the leadership role she had played in the church where my cousin Kim was the worship leader and her husband was the pastor. I knew this loss was going to be very difficult, not only for my mom but also for my ninety-year-old grandmother. Mom had moved her from Orlando to Panama City after my grandfather had passed away a year before my aunt was diagnosed with cancer.

Known as Big Daddy, my grandfather was the funniest man who ever graced this planet. In fact, we all said it wouldn't be heaven unless Big Daddy was there. He made every day a fun day, no matter what the circumstance or what the task at hand might be. Unfortunately, he didn't become a Christian until he was diagnosed with colon cancer. Mom and I had the awesome privilege of leading him to the Lord.

I'll never forget the night Mom and I talked before bed one night. We decided we weren't leaving the following day without sealing the deal, which meant the next day was Big Daddy's day for salvation. Right after breakfast the next morning Mom and I asked him to come sit on the couch while Mimi, my grandmother, washed the dishes. Mimi had been saved for years, so she was thrilled for us to talk and pray with Big Daddy. Mom had shared the love of God with him many times before, but he would usually make jokes and say that Lady Luck had served him well over the years.

Big Daddy was the baby of ten children. He'd taken care of himself through the Great Depression and had lived to tell war stories, including what he had witnessed of the Holocaust. Now, with cancer weakening his body, the once independent, self-sufficient, successful entrepreneur was in need of a power higher than himself.

After Mom shared her heart about his condition and his need for a Savior, I took Big Daddy's hands and asked him to repeat after me. He was slow to repeat, but he asked Jesus into his heart that morning. Mom and I left feeling overwhelmingly joyful about his decision. We got into Mom's car, opened the sunroof, and played praise music all the way home. Since Mom had become a Christian, she had prayed faithfully for her family to come to know the Lord. It was because of her diligence to seek Him that her prayers had been answered, just as it says in the Bible: "The effective, fervent prayer of a righteous man avails much" (James 5:16, NKJV).

Sion and I made the long journey back to Texas, and once we arrived, Mom left immediately for Panama City. Since flying was not going to allow Mom and her husband, Jerry, enough time to be there for the viewing, they decided to make the six-hour drive to Orlando the same day Mom flew in from Texas. My grandmother had recently been diagnosed with arthritis and was in so much pain from the spurs pressing on the spine that she was unable to make the car trip. Mom arranged for the caretaker to stay longer until she returned from the funeral.

Mom was feeling the pressures of life on all sides, yet she remained strong and full of faith, knowing that the Bible says, "And without faith it is impossible to please God, because anyone who comes to him must believe that he exists and that he rewards those who earnestly seek him" (Heb. 11:6).

About forty-five minutes into their drive, they encountered car trouble, and Mom called Stacey to come and get them. Jerry noticed the check engine light had come on in his Tahoe and didn't want to risk driving any farther, especially since they would be arriving in Orlando at midnight. The plan was to leave the vehicle where it was, return to the house and get the other car, and then continue to Orlando.

When Stacey arrived to pick them up, Mom noticed that her skin color didn't look right. Knowing Stacey was on medication for her blood pressure, Mom asked if she was feeling OK. Stacey told her she was fine, but that didn't stop Mom from fussing at her for not eating right and reminding her that smoking was bad for her and the children's health. Once they'd returned to the house and were ready to leave, Mom gave Stacey a hug and thanked her for picking them up. Then she turned to her and tenderly said, "Stacey, take care of yourself."

Stacey then took a deep breath as if she couldn't hold her excitement back any longer and told Mom that the guy she'd been dating over the last year had asked her to marry him.

"Do the children know about this?" Mom asked with great concern.

"No, not yet," she replied. "We're planning a family dinner with the children and will let them know of our marriage plans." The children had already grown accustomed to the new gentleman and had spent time camping and visiting his parents' farm on different occasions. My mom had no idea that their relationship had become so serious. She didn't have time to dive deeper into the discussion, so she quickly hugged Stacey again and said, "I'll call you when I return on Wednesday evening so you can tell me more."

That was the last time my mom saw Stacey alive. She died sometime during the night on May 14, just hours after my mom had returned from my aunt's funeral.

What do you do when life caves in unexpectedly? My mom found refuge in God's Word, which says, "They who seek the Lord will praise him" (Ps. 22:26).

We can't survive without Him. God desires for us to *seek Him.*

Chapter 4

LOVE HIM

I COULDN'T BELIEVE THAT, for the second time in only three years, our family was returning to Panama City for yet another funeral. As hard as this was on us, I couldn't even begin to imagine how Stacey's children must be feeling after first losing Michael, their father, and now their mother. The older children, Elizabeth (age fifteen), Mary Catherine (age fourteen), and Emily (age eleven), were likely in shock. As for David (age eight) and Caroline (age four), they would undoubtedly draw comfort from their older sisters.

It was well past midnight when we got to my mom's house and used the key she'd left under the mat to let ourselves in. When we woke up late the next morning, Mom filled me in on everything that had happened over the previous twenty-four hours.

Stacey's weekday habit was to rise early and turn on her radio while she dressed for work. Elizabeth was usually the first child to get up in the morning, but she had slept in because she stayed up late talking with her mom. Mary Catherine woke up as the sun was peeking through the blinds, and when she didn't hear the radio, she assumed her mom had overslept. She is the one who found her mother unconscious on the bed that morning.

Knowing something was terribly wrong, Mary Catherine went immediately to awaken her older sister Elizabeth, who knew CPR. Elizabeth did everything she'd been trained to do while Mary Catherine called Stacey's brother Dan, who was a local paramedic. When Dan and his wife, Mindy, arrived, he quickly determined that his sister had passed away. While Mindy comforted the two girls, Dan began making the necessary phone calls.

Stacey's third daughter, Emily, was in Saint Augustine with her fifth-grade class and would not be home until the following day. David and Caroline were upstairs sleeping until David was awakened by the sound of his sisters crying in the hallway. From the moment Elizabeth told him what had happened, he clung to her for support, choosing not to go into the room to see his mother. Mercifully, little Caroline slept through the whole process.

As I said in the last chapter, we each handle grief in our own way, and so it was with the children. Always the picture of responsibility, fifteen-year-old Elizabeth decided that she wanted to go to school that morning. At her age she probably knew that she would find comfort in being with her friends. Mary Catherine and David stayed home with their aunt and uncle. And Caroline, who was excited about her graduation that evening from her Little Lambs preschool, was taken to school by one of Stacey's close friends. As it turned out, the last communication my mom had from Stacey was a voice message about that graduation, a message that Mom played for Sion and me as we sat together at the breakfast table that morning.

"Hi, Honey," we heard Stacey's familiar voice say,

referring to my mom by her "grandmother" name, Honey. "Just wanted to let you know that Caroline graduates from Little Lambs tomorrow night at seven. We're looking forward to seeing you there." Realizing that only hours after she'd left this message for my mom, Stacey was gone, I wept at the thought of how fragile life can be and how a single, unexpected event can alter the course of destiny for so many.

Sion and I were exhausted from the previous day's thirteen-hour drive, so it was noon before we arrived at Stacey's house to assess what needed to be done and determine how we could help. Stacey's brother and his wife had gone to meet Emily, who would be returning with her classmates from the bus trip to Saint Augustine. They had the unenviable job of telling her about her mother. My dad had accompanied Stacey's mother to make the funeral arrangements, and several of Stacey's other siblings were already at the home when we arrived. The children were happy to see us and for the most part were responsive to us and to our being there. The exceptions were Elizabeth, the oldest, and Caroline, the youngest.

Elizabeth had steeled herself to the trauma she was experiencing and preferred the company of her friends to that of her family. Whenever any of us would attempt to talk to her and comfort her, she was stiff and unresponsive. Because four-year-old Caroline had been born after we were already in Texas, she was not as familiar with Sion and me as she was with her other aunts and uncles, which was understandable. When I introduced myself as her daddy's sister, she showed more interest in getting to know me. I was related to the man she'd loved seeing in family photos and whom she'd heard so many stories about. Mary Catherine and David immediately engaged with us, telling us about everything that was going on in their lives and asking if we'd all go to the beach again this summer as we'd done in years past. Following our annual trip to the beach the previous summer, David had returned to Texas and stayed with us for four weeks. I wasn't surprised when he asked, "Aunt Shannon, are you going to come get me again this summer?"

"I sure am," I said with a smile. Of course, I didn't have a clue how we were going to work it out.

Emily, who had returned from her fifth grade trip to St. Augustine, was playing at her best friend's house. I tried to keep up a positive conversation with Mary Catherine since she seemed the most subdued about the events of the day.

"So I heard you swam today," I said to her.

"Yeah, I can't believe I won," she responded with a grin.

Mary Catherine had started swimming in the sixth grade, and she currently swam for the middle school she'd attended for the past two years. Her mom had been quite proud of her, but her dad never had the opportunity to see her swim on a team. She was very competitive and had done well the entire year.

The day she woke up and found her mom dead, she had a county swim meet scheduled for that afternoon. She went with her aunt that morning to get out of the house before the paramedics came to pick her mom up. Then later her aunt took her to the county swim meet. She went to her warm-up practice, and her coach asked if she was sure she wanted to swim. Mary Catherine nodded her head and asked that she not tell anyone what had happened. Her coach hugged her and allowed her to prepare for the meet as planned. She told her coach she had all intentions of not quitting but doing her best in the meet.

Mary Catherine had two nicknames her daddy had given her. He called her "MC" because when she was a toddler, none of the cousins could say Mary Catherine. It sounded more like "moey calfrin," so MC had made it much easier. Then as she'd grown older, her dad called her "Chick" because all she wanted to eat was chicken.

Although one of Stacey's sisters took MC to the meet that day, there was one more family member who offered support as she carried out the scheduled plans. My dad met her there. It was his first time seeing her swim. He told her he would buy a chicken nugget meal at Sonic as a reward if she swam well.

When it was her time to compete, he yelled, "Do it for your mom!" The buzzer went off, and though she wasn't the first one in the water, Dad screamed, "Go, Chick!" with tears running down his face. The *Chariots of Fire* music began. She beat her time and won both the fifty-yard breaststroke and the fifty-yard backstroke that day. The place went crazy, because in our small town, almost everyone knew what that child had been through.

Sometimes it takes walking through difficult situations to realize that people are more important than anything else in life. My dad told me he was so thankful to be there to encourage Mary Catherine and support the daughter of the son he wished could still be standing by his side.

Hebrews 3:13 says, "But encourage one another daily, as long as it is called Today." No one is promised tomorrow, but God encourages us to love Him and others today. Don't miss these opportunities—love Him!

The following day Stacey's brother and his wife arrived from South Florida. They were the couple who had been named as alternate guardians for the children.

Now all of Stacey's siblings, her two brothers and her two sisters, were either at the house caring for the children or staying nearby. My cousin had flown in from Pittsburg, and she was staying with my grandmother. She was a huge help in keeping Stacey's house organized and in running off the children's friends at night so that the household could get a good night's rest. I merely assisted her as I tried connecting with all the children.

Stacey's mother, who'd been widowed many years earlier when her six children were young, had since married a retired military pilot. She lived only a few minutes away and dropped by from time to time. She mainly took care of the viewing and funeral arrangements. Many people brought food by the house, so no one went hungry, including the neighbors.

The weekend was a flurry of activity as we made preparation for Monday's funeral service while trying to coordinate the care of Stacey's five grieving children. The bigger question that loomed before us was how we would care for the children once we got past their mother's funeral. All I could think about was the meeting we'd had with Michael and Stacey just a little over three years prior, when Sion and I had said we'd take all five children should the unthinkable happen.

Well, it had just happened.

Our finances were stable, and we lived in a nice house, but it was a four-bedroom, three-bathroom house—one that hadn't sold in the three years it had been on the market, I reminded myself. Each of my children had been living in their own space for the last two years. The boys shared a bathroom, while Brooke had a bathroom to herself. I couldn't imagine the rivalry we would have with five girls sharing the same bathroom.

"Mom, I don't know what we're going to do," I confided one morning when Sion and I were talking with her. "Our kids don't know anything about the commitment we made to Michael and Stacey, and I doubt that their kids or anyone other than Stacey's brother and his wife from South Florida know about it either. How are we going to tell them?"

"Shannon," my mom said, "Stacey's brothers and sisters are at the house comforting the children. They are OK now, but we need to think about what we need to do from this point forward. The first thing we all need to do is come together as a family and decide what's best for the children."

Mom went on to say that she didn't have a copy of Michael and Stacey's will, and neither did Stacey's mother. She had already contacted the attorney who'd drawn up the document, and he would have copies ready for her to pick up first thing Monday morning.

"OK then," Sion said. "There's nothing anyone can do until we have a copy of the will, so let's just focus on the kids."

"Right," my mom said. "The best thing the two of you can do right now is just be there for them."

As I looked at all of the people who'd gathered after the funeral service to show their support for Michael and Stacey's children, I couldn't help but think how blessed they were to have so many friends and family members who loved them. I was also thankful that their parents had made the decision to put their wishes regarding the children's care in writing. It would make the process we were about to go through easier for everyone.

Sion and I sat down with my mother that night, and for the first time we saw the document that had been drawn up three years earlier naming us as guardians. I was confident in my ability to form a plan for taking care of the children once they were with us, but I didn't have a clue about what it would take to go through the legal process of making it happen. The wisdom and tenacity it was going to take to walk through the process would come from Mom and Sion. The responsibility and discipline it was going to take to run the ship efficiently would come from me. But more importantly we knew it was ultimately going to take the love of God to win this battle and make a new beginning of rearing eight children a beautiful thing. We were all in need of the grace to walk out what the apostle Paul had written about love. "Love is patient, love is kind. It does not envy, it does not boast, it is not proud. It is not rude, it is not self-seeking, it is not easily angered, it keeps no record of wrongs. Love does not delight in evil, but rejoices with the truth. It always protects, always trusts, always hopes, always perseveres. Love never fails" (1 Cor. 13:4–8).

This is one of my favorite passages in the Bible because

God gives us an absolute. In other words, love wins every fight or battle we face. Our responsibility is to walk in love, and when we do, love defeats the darkness and never fails us. I know God wants us to love Him as well as encourage our children, knowing love is the key to unlocking many other promises He has given us.

The Word of God tells us, "Love the Lord your God with all your heart and with all your soul and with all your strength. These commandments that I give you today are to be upon your hearts. Impress them on your children. Talk about them when you sit at home and when you walk along the road, when you lie down and when you get up. Tie them as symbols on your hands and bind them on your foreheads. Write them on the doorframes of your houses and on your gates" (Deut. 6:5–9).

These two scriptures became my reference point for the battles ahead.

One concern my mom shared with us that evening was the fact that only Michael's signature was on the document. The attorney explained that Stacey was unavailable to come with Michael the day he signed the document. Her intention was to return to add her signature later, but that's when Michael began to decline rapidly and she never returned.

"Both the attorney and I were there when Stacey made her wishes known about not splitting up the children," Mom said. "She was so adamant about it that I'm sure she must have told her mother...and probably her brother and sister-in-law from South Florida since they are named as alternate guardians. I guess we'll find out for sure once we all sit down together."

My dad is the one who made the arrangements for

the family to discuss Michael and Stacey's will after the funeral. The reason we met at this time was, as horrible and emotionally raw as everything was about Stacey's sudden death, Sion and I had to leave the next day to return to work and our children had to return to school. Everyone agreed to meet at Dad's office, since it offered a neutral environment. It was my understanding that Mom, Dad, Sion, and I would be meeting with Stacey's mom and the alternate guardians, Stacey's brother and sister-in-law. I was surprised when Stacey's mom arrived, accompanied by all four of her children, their spouses, and other distant relatives by marriage. We literally ran out of seats and left standing room only for all the other unexpected company.

It was Stacey's brother Dan who acted as the family's spokesperson that day. He let us know that he and his wife had temporarily moved into Stacey's house in order to be there for the children until they finished school in three weeks. Other family members and two of Stacey's friends would be working with them to make sure the kids got to school and to their various activities. Knowing that the children's immediate needs would be met, we then moved on to the will.

My dad explained that prior to Michael's death and subsequent to Stacey's heart attack, they had gone to an attorney who had drawn up a will naming Shannon and Sion as guardians for the children. Stacey's brother and his wife from South Florida were named as alternate guardians. He then presented a copy to Stacey's mother.

After she and Dan read the document, they pointed out that Stacey's signature did not appear on the will. They said that without her signature, it was not her will.

Dan said their family was concerned about how difficult it would be for any one family to assume the responsibility of all five children. He felt the best solution was for the children to move in with different family members who lived in Panama City so that they could remain close to each other.

My mom told everyone about the meeting Michael and Stacey had with Sion and me at her home, where they asked us if we were willing to be named as guardians for all five children. She also explained that she had accompanied Michael and Stacey to meet with the attorney and that Stacey had been adamant about the children not being split up.

It was understandable that Stacey's family did not like the idea of the children leaving Florida to move to Texas. Another concern they had was their perception of instability in our lives, since they assumed that Sion was still traveling in ministry. We assured them that Sion had been steadily employed for more than a year at a job that provided medical benefits, which would be extended to the children as well. We also assured them that we were prepared to take all five children in order to keep them together in accordance with their parents' wishes.

I do not doubt that every one of us gathered in that room that day was there because of our shared love for Elizabeth, Mary Catherine, Emily, David, and Caroline and our desire to do what was best for them. However, our ideas about what was best for them were radically different. Dan said he would be willing to move into Stacey's house permanently if that's what it took to keep them together in Florida. The other siblings agreed they'd do what they could to help. On the other hand, my mom continued to point to Michael and Stacey's will and their expressed wish that Sion and I be named the children's guardians.

Sion spoke up and said, "These children are living in a home where they lost a ten-day-old brother from a heart murmur, a father from cancer, and now their mom from a heart attack. I think they need a fresh start, and living in the same environment would only remind them of pain and what they have lost."

After a tension-filled meeting that lasted over two hours, we decided to take things one step at a time. Because Stacey's brother and his wife from South Florida, who had been named alternate guardians, had to return to their home and jobs, Dan and his wife, Mindy, moved into the house so that the kids could finish school. I would return to Panama City the first week in June, and we would work together to come up with a plan for the summer.

During the next three weeks the two oldest children, Elizabeth and Mary Catherine, stayed with friends at their houses. Emily stayed with Stacey's friend Betsy, leaving Dan and his wife in charge of only David and Caroline, the two youngest children. Stacey's sisters and friends helped with getting them to their activities.

My mom stayed in touch with Dan on a regular basis and kept me advised about how things were proceeding. Because Panama City was a small town and Dan was active in the community, he was able to talk to someone at the local Social Security office to arrange drawing benefits for the children even without a legal document showing guardianship. The dental office where Stacey worked allowed him to pick up her final check, which he cashed so that he could begin sorting through bills to figure out where she was financially. Meanwhile Mom owned the house Dan and the children were living in and understood probate laws and the procedures that needed to take place to liquidate items and pay off the mounting bills.

Both Mom and Dan were trying to help the children, but they were separately working against each other with strained communication. They had different opinions of what was best for the children. The result was a two-headed monster, and it seemed the only way to resolve the issues was to go to court. The children were in the middle of all the tension and miscommunication, and it only made matters worse each time the idea of moving to Texas came up. Needless to say, it was a difficult time for the two families to show each other love, with five children in the middle of adults playing tug-of-war.

In one of the discussions Dan had with my mom, the subject of Michael and Stacey's house came up. When he didn't find any checks written to a mortgage company while he was going through Stacey's bank statements, he'd assumed that the house was paid for. His thought was to rent out his house and move permanently into Stacey's home with the children. My mom had no choice at that point but to disclose the circumstances leading to her carrying the note on the house.

Needless to say, the knowledge that my mother owned the house only added further stress to an already tense relationship between the two sides of the family.

As planned, I returned to Panama City in early June. Sion did not need to take more time off from work, but Si, Brooke, and Austin were all too happy to have the opportunity to see their cousins again so soon.

Mom had arranged for Elizabeth, Mary Catherine, Emily, David, and Caroline to spend some time at her house. Once we arrived, all eight of the kids were together again under one roof. Just as they had each summer when we visited, the kids enjoyed swimming and playing together. One night, after everyone had had their fill of s'mores and the younger children were in bed, Mom and I called the four oldest children together. My own Si and Brooke, along with their cousins Elizabeth and Mary Catherine, listened intently as my mother began to speak to them.

Looking at Elizabeth and Mary Catherine, Mom said, "I want to share with you what your mom and dad's wishes are concerning your care."

Mom talked to them about what was in the document and then handed it to the girls so that they could process it. After a few moments both of them began to cry. Addressing my mom by their pet name for her, they said, "But, Honey, we don't want to leave Florida. We don't want to leave our friends. We love our cousins, but we don't want to live thirteen hours away from our home."

Si and Brooke knew of the plans for their cousins to be with us in Texas during the summer, but this was the first time they'd heard that the arrangement might be permanent. Sion and I had been careful not to discuss the matter in front of them. They too got to read the will and see it for themselves.

Thinking that there must have been a mistake, Elizabeth and Mary Catherine could not accept the idea that their parents would have wanted them to leave Florida. My mother was so patient with them, showing them the date of the document and reminding them that Sion and I already lived in Texas at the time the will was drawn up.

She also addressed the idea that some members of the family felt that the document didn't represent Stacey's wishes because she didn't return to sign it. "Elizabeth and Mary Catherine, I was there in the lawyer's office. I heard the conversation your parents had with the attorney, and it *was* your mom's wishes. She does not want you to be split up. If you stay here in Florida, you'd be living in different places; you would not all be together."

"That's fine. As long as we're here with our friends, the other ones can go to different places," Elizabeth said. Mary Catherine agreed.

"You girls need to think past yourselves; don't be selfish about this. Let's think this thing through, because months from now you may regret that you're not all together. There may be times when you draw strength from each other, especially the younger children." Looking directly at Elizabeth, she added, "It would be almost like another death to Emily, David, and Caroline for you to say, 'I'm staying in Florida; you can take them.' It would be so much easier for them if you all stay together."

That's when I added, "In three years, Elizabeth, you will be graduating from high school and stepping into college. That will be the natural process for you to leave, and we'll celebrate your coming home."

Mary Catherine looked at me and said, "I'll go with

you for the summer, Aunt Shannon, but I want to come back here when school starts."

Elizabeth remained adamant. "I am *not* leaving Florida. I'm staying here with my friends. Besides, I already made color guard for next year at Bay High School, and I'm going to camp this summer."

Mom knew when it was time to say goodnight. She told the girls that everyone on both sides of the family wanted to do what was best for them and their younger siblings. She assured them there was still a lot of time before final decisions had to be made.

After Si, Brooke, Elizabeth, and Mary Catherine went to bed that night, Mom turned her attention to me. "Shannon, just give the situation some time where Elizabeth and Mary Catherine are concerned. Let me talk to them about the legal issues. You focus on being there for them and letting them know how much you care. You are a wonderful mother to your own children, and I know you'll be just as wonderful to them as well. Now you go get some rest; you've got a busy day with the kids tomorrow."

"But, Mom, how am I going to convince them they will love Texas and find wonderful friends there too when they keep telling me they don't want to go no matter what I do for them?" I said with a sigh.

Mom wrapped her arms around me and said, "Don't you worry. If God can change the heart of Pharaoh, God can change the hearts of these frightened, unleashed teenagers."

"Thanks, Mom. I love you."

"I love you too."

As I lay in bed that night thinking about what my mom had said about my being a wonderful mother, my mind went back to the words the pastor spoke over me at the presbytery at Gateway Church: "'You are an excellent, an extreme mom, and an extremely good mom.' The Lord wants to confirm this to you as a calling to you in your life, that the greatest thing that you will *ever do* is what you're *already doing* as a mother, that you were needed there and you were called there."

"What person doesn't like being needed?" I thought. "I have the need to be needed. It makes me feel loved, but how can I possibly meet all those needs? We are going to be responsible for shaping eight lives."

This calling was too much and at times almost felt confining. The apostle Paul must have felt the same way as he wrote an encouraging prophetic note to the church, telling us how to walk worthy of high position:

> In light of all this, here's what I want you to do. While I'm locked up here, a prisoner for the Master, I want you to get out there and walk—better yet, run!—on the road God called you to travel. I don't want any of you sitting around on your hands. I don't want anyone strolling off, down some path that goes nowhere. And mark that you do this with humility and discipline—not in fits and starts, but steadily, pouring yourselves out for each other in acts of love, alert at noticing differences and quick at mending fences.
>
> —EPHESIANS 4:1–3, THE MESSAGE

I drifted off to sleep that night with the assurance that God would be with me as I walked through this next transition in my life. I know the answer to this prayer. God wants me to *love Him*.

Sion & Shannon Alford married May 15, 1992

Michael & Stacey Schwartz married June 15, 1990

Sion & Shannon Alford wedding matron of honor, maid of honor, bridesmaids, best man and groomsmen

Sion & Shannon in Israel looking over Jerusalem

Soda can wars are a must for blended families to bond together as one.

Alford/Schwartz family's first day of school picture taken after supper

At last, in our new home eating at the table where everyone can share about their day.

BNHS Color Guard team – Elizabeth with her best friend, Brittany, she met the first day of school.

Front cover of our first Christmas card as one big family (2009) "Psalm 5:11"

Back cover of our 2009 Christmas card as one big family

Our first Christmas in 2009 and my brother's children's first time seeing and playing in the snow.

"Army of One" band, only in concert for holidays and family gatherings.

I asked a lady while walking out of the driver's license office to take our picture as I kissed and squeezed Elizabeth. This was a monumental moment for both of us. God is faithful!!

Eighties night youth group party with friends

Merry Christmas

The Alfords

2010 front cover Christmas card picture "Psalm 127:3-5"

2010 back cover Christmas card picture

Mary Catherine's Sweet "16" Party with her best friend Kate and other friends from school.

Mary Catherine swimming butterfly for Byron Nelson High School.

Si playing baseball for Byron Nelson High School.

Elizabeth in the medical academy at Byron Nelson High School.

Elizabeth leading worship in kids church at Gateway Church.

David and "Pops" 5th grade science project knocked it out of the park.

2011 Christmas card picture taken at Sea Grove Beach near Panama City known as the "world's most beautiful beach" in Florida. "Psalm 113:3"

2011 inside cover of our Christmas Card

Hanging on the wall of our home, our lives are represented as a cross under submission to His cross and life.

Sion and I led worship at our North Richland Hills Campus on Easter 2012.

Austin received a most valuable player for tennis. Look out ESPN!!

Caroline received an award for playing soccer, her first team sport. Sweet!!

Si was awarded the "Leadership" award from Byron Nelson High School. To God be the Glory!!

My Dad enjoying a grandfather moment pointing out Mary Catherine's swim achievements.

Brooke and Emily cheering for Byron Nelson High School. Super Cute!!

Elizabeth's graduation at Byron Nelson High School, class of 2012 is the first graduating class. What a very special honor!

Chapter 5

HONOR HIM

THE NEXT DAY was Caroline's fifth birthday. As Mom and I had a cup of coffee and shared an early morning breakfast alone, we discussed the plans for the day.

"Shannon, I think we had enough last night of trying to explain the situation. Let's don't bring anything up today. Instead we'll just have fun."

The community in which she lived was near the beach. Sion's dad, Mr. Alford, had given me a key to a large community pool at Rosemary Beach. I had taken the children there during spring break when we wanted a variety of water fun activities.

Mom said, "Take the kids to the beach. Then have a fun birthday celebration at the community pool."

"OK, Mom, good idea. But what should I feed them for lunch?"

I knew I needed to fill them up before all of the activities, and snacks wouldn't do the trick. My new group was hungry every hour, and I had to have eight of every snack, or there would be wars and rumors of wars.

"I'll take them to Burger King so they can each have it their way and get what they want," I decided.

We both laughed as the baby birds with pillow-head

hairdos began to surface from what appeared a good night's rest.

Mom packed a beach bag with some of the items we'd need for our afternoon at the pool, and as soon as everyone was ready, we were off to Burger King to begin our celebration of Caroline's big day. We ate our lunch together in the picnic area by the pool, where I took a great photo of the cousins enjoying their day together. Anyone who saw them laughing and playing would never have suspected that some of them had just suffered the loss of their mother. Yet as I looked into the eyes of the older children, there was no hiding the grief that had befallen them.

Caroline was thoroughly enjoying all of the attention she was receiving, and I was happy that she interacted with me without reservation. While her siblings had spent their early years getting to know me as their Aunt Shannon, whose house was located just a few miles from their own, Caroline had not shared that experience. Sion and the kids and I had left Panama City before she was born, and she was still trying to grasp our relationship.

"So, you're my dad's sister, right?" she would ask again and again with her inquisitive smile. And I'd always reply, "Yes, I'm your dad's sister," knowing she was so young when Michael died that she didn't have any actual memory of him. Thinking of how I wished that things could have turned out differently for all of us, I could hear my brother's famous words, "Well, it is what it is!" In other words, don't allow the situation to pull you down; just make the most of your day. That's when I would tell her a story about him and make her laugh, hoping Michael was able to peek over the clouds and see his little girl on her fifth birthday.

As soon as lunch was over, the kids formed their usual groups and were off to play and swim while I stayed with Caroline in the kiddie pool. She was surprisingly independent, being the youngest child. She didn't hesitate to let me know that she could do everything the older kids could do, but there was no way I was going to leave her side. Besides, I found her childlike candor thoroughly charming and couldn't wait to hear what she was going to say next.

In the beach bag Mom had sent with me that day were some toys Caroline particularly enjoyed playing with. She invented a game where I threw the toys into the water and she would "swim" to get them and return them to me. I marveled at how God had arranged this time for us to spend together so that we could develop a relationship.

Pretty soon Caroline noticed another little girl about her age whose mother was also throwing toys. In no time Caroline and the little girl became friends. They decided it would be fun if the girl's mother and I tossed the toys at the same time so that they could have a contest to see who returned their toy first.

When the other little girl shouted to Caroline, "Tell your mom to hurry up and throw the ring," I felt myself stiffen as I waited to see how Caroline would respond.

Without batting an eye, Caroline turned and said, "She's not my mom. My mom died." Then she jumped into the pool and started doing back flips. This was my first time doing anything alone with my niece, and despite the fact that she was known for her undiluted honesty, I was still caught off guard. "Oh my word," I thought as I realized that if you want to know something, just ask Caroline. From that point on I knew that we were going to share a very special relationship.

I already had a solid relationship with both Emily and David. Their hugs were heartfelt and filled with warmth, and they always spoke endearingly when they called me Aunt Shannon. But although the older girls, Elizabeth and Mary Catherine, were always kind and respectful, it was apparent to all of us that they'd been hardened by the trauma they'd experienced over the past three years. First they'd lost a brother. Then they'd lost their father and gone through the inevitable ensuing transition in their home life. And finally they'd suffered the loss of their mother.

Both girls struggled to be independent, especially Elizabeth, who felt the pressure and responsibility of raising her younger siblings. Although she'd had the support of adult family members in the weeks following Stacey's death, she had nonetheless taken on the role of mother to the other children. It was clearly a role she was not mature enough to assume. Mom and I were concerned for her as we saw the self-imposed burden she was carrying.

We decided that while the kids were with us for the next couple of weeks, I would focus on being a mother to them. In the familiar comfort of their grandmother's home, I would see to it that all of their daily needs were met. Our hope was that by my handling all of the cooking, cleaning, laundry, and care of the younger children, Elizabeth would realize that she could be a child herself. We wanted her just to enjoy being with her siblings before she and Emily left for their summer camps.

While the older children stayed in touch with Stacey's brothers and sisters and kept them informed about our daily plans and activities, my mom was communicating with Stacey's mother about the long-term plans. We had hoped that with some passing of time since the funeral, she would agree to honor Michael and Stacey's wishes for the children to live with us. Sadly that hadn't happened.

"Shannon, both your dad and I have talked with Stacey's mom about settling the issue with the children, but she doesn't want them to leave Florida," my mom told me. "As their grandmother, I can certainly understand how she feels. We've explained that going to court will be both an expensive and combative process for everyone, which can be avoided if she will just sign a document acknowledging you and Sion as the guardians named in the will."

"Do you think she's going to do that, Mom? I hate the idea of having to go to court."

"I don't know, Shannon, but you let me and your dad worry about that. For now, why don't you think about taking Mary Catherine, David, and Caroline back to Texas for a while since Elizabeth and Emily are away at camp?"

My fortieth birthday was in a couple of days, and I really wanted to be home with Sion to celebrate, so we talked to the kids and told them we'd be leaving for Texas on the thirteenth. Si, Brooke, and Austin were thrilled that their cousins would be returning with us. From their perspective it was going to be a summer of endless fun. For me, I knew God was giving me small doses of this medicine so that I could adjust to six children before I was given the whole bottle.

"God, You know me," I prayed. "I love to entertain, but not all the time. I like everything neat and orderly, and my children are accustomed to a tight ship. How am I going to adjust to the clutter and noise until my brother's children adapt to our environment?"

Gently I heard Him say, "Honor one another."

I was surprised to learn that the saying "cleanliness is next to godliness" is not in the Bible, but I knew that the Book of Romans had something to say about honoring one another: "Be devoted to one another in brotherly love. Honor one another above yourselves. Never be lacking in zeal, but keep your spiritual fervor, serving the Lord. Be joyful in hope, patient in affliction, faithful in prayer. Share with God's people who are in need. Practice hospitality" (Rom. 12:10–13).

As the character Sully taught us in the amazing Pixar movie *Monsters, Inc.*, children are not creatures but little people. My new little people needed me to love and honor them for who they were. Yes, it was important to establish rules, chore schedules, and procedures, but most of all they needed me to relax and know this melding together as one family was going to take time. And what a patient God we serve. He wants us to honor Him by honoring others above ourselves.

We had packed the minivan the previous night, so all we had to do on the thirteenth was just get in and go. At six thirty the next morning we were standing in the driveway saying our final good-byes to my mom when a police car pulled up.

The officer approached me and said, "I'm sorry, ma'am, but we received a report that you are attempting to take these children out of state without any documentation."

I was too stunned to speak—but my mother wasn't. "Officer, I am the grandmother of all six of these children. This woman is my daughter. Her brother passed away three years ago from cancer, and we just lost his wife when she suffered a heart attack. If you'll excuse me for a minute, I'll provide you with the documentation."

After a few awkward minutes Mom returned with a copy of the will. She went on to explain, "My son and his wife had five children. Two of them are at camp, and my daughter is going to take three of them with her for the summer until a court date is set. That's all she is doing. Here's a copy of the will naming her and her husband as guardians."

After reading the will, the officer handed it back to my mother and then turned to me and said, "Whoa, I'm so sorry for the inconvenience, ma'am. You can go ahead and leave now...and please drive safely."

After getting off to an eventful and challenging start, we were on our way back to Texas. I had six kids ranging in age from five to fifteen years with me, and we must have looked like a can of sardines traveling down the highway on a set of four wheels. After thirteen hours and two pit stops, we arrived early that evening, tired but happy to be home.

Home. How was I ever going to fit five more children into our house? I sent up a silent prayer: "Please, Lord, bring a buyer for this house."

We quickly established a workable sleeping arrangement for the kids. David joined Austin in his room, where they spent countless hours playing together as they'd done the previous summer. The arrangement was a little more of a stretch for Brooke, who was accustomed to her own bedroom and bathroom, but she was willing to share her space with Mary Catherine and Caroline, especially since at that point it was only going to be for a few weeks. Si continued to sleep in the guestroom as he had been doing since the beginning of middle school.

My mom and I talked almost daily. She told me that when Elizabeth and Emily returned from their summer camps, Elizabeth wanted to stay at a friend's house. Their uncle from South Florida invited Emily to stay with his family until the issue with guardianship was decided. Their Uncle Dan allowed them to do so while he and his wife remained in Stacey's house. While we were both concerned that Elizabeth was not being parented, we knew both girls were safe. We didn't want to create an issue that would only add further animosity to the situation.

Sion and I kept up our end of the agreement by focusing on nurturing Mary Catherine, David, and Caroline, while Mom and my dad worked together to try to resolve the guardianship issue with Stacey's family.

I had maintained hope that Mom's appeal to Stacey's mother to abide by Stacey and Michael's wishes would be successful. But when she told my mom that she'd turned the matter over to her son Dan, I knew that the already fragile situation was likely to turn sour.

Although Dan was aware that my mother owned the house he and his wife had recently moved into, he informed Mom that his intention was to stay there and seek to keep the kids in Florida. That's when Mom made one last appeal directly to Dan.

"As much as I love the children and as much as their grandfather loves them, we know that the best thing we can do on their behalf is release them to go to Texas with Shannon and Sion," she said. "There is so much more for them there, and it would be an opportunity for them to have a fresh start."

Mom was adamant in her belief that being with Sion and me was what was best for the children. Dan was equally adamant that it would be better not to uproot them from Florida, even though they would be living with different relatives within the state. Both arguments stemmed from love and were valid where the children's well-being was concerned. Unfortunately, it was now apparent that the issue of guardianship would have to be decided by a court. My mother retained an attorney, Dan retained an attorney, and a court date was set for July 15, less than one month away.

"What is the point of a will if you don't honor the wishes of the one who signed it?" I asked my mom on the phone. "Can't Stacey's family see that Michael and Stacey had no intentions of the children staying in Panama City, Florida? They both knew where we lived, and if they hadn't wanted them to move to Texas, they wouldn't have placed us as their first choice. The will wasn't made based on what state they lived in, but on who had them and the desire that they all would stay together."

"Yes, I agree," sighed Mom. "Don't worry, I've been in touch with every person I can remember whom Michael and Stacey shared their desires about their children with. They are all willing to either testify in court or write a letter to my attorney stating the facts."

This was a letter written to honor my brother and sister-in-law's desires:

7/6/2009

To whom it may concern:

I was disappointed to hear of the conflict over custody of the Schwartz children. However, little can intensify the emotions of so many as do our beliefs about the well-being of our children. No doubt all parties are convinced in their own mind about the better welfare of the children in question.

I was asked to write to you a statement of what I knew of Michael Schwartz and his relations to his children, as well as other relevant information that emerged in my ministry to the family.

First, let me say a little of what I know about Michael Schwartz as a man and father. He began attending Lynn Haven Methodist in January of 2005, joined in March of 2005, and was in active attendance until his death in June 2006. Both Stacey and Michael volunteered in the nursery and in some youth capacities during that time. Overall, during their time here, they were very engaged and active members. I saw him frequently, and he and I had several conversations before his sickness began, after which time we were in contact more often.

My evaluation of the kind of man Michael was is very positive. He appeared both at church and at home to be a very attentive, gracious, and engaged father. Both in his home and at church his children constantly gravitated toward him, and there seemed to be a very high level of appropriate child-parent intimacy. At church the family always appeared together, and Michael was fully integrated into their comings, movements, and goings.

While in their home for visits during Michael's illness, his children often interrupted us to talk to him, show him things, or to sit on his lap or hug him. Stacey apologized on a number of occasions for these frequent interruptions in our conversation, but they were, of course, no bother. I even witnessed some very difficult moments when his cancer made using his lap or giving a hug very painful for him. It was evident that he constantly went out of his way to be a nurturing figure. One time this was particularly evident in conversation was when he talked about his son that had died after only ten days. The anguish of the loss that still hurt him so deeply was a testimony to the deep connection and love he had for his children—even those lost.

On one occasion Stacey, Michael, and I talked about some family tension over Michael's choice to be more of a family man than a businessman. This had apparently caused some disappointment in his wider family, over which he was remorseful, but both very much confirmed their choices to be primarily family people. Stacey expressed, on a number of (several of which were not in his presence) occasions, lavish praise about Michael's fathering and his choice to prioritize family over career.

Also, I saw nothing in the Schwartz children that would lead me to believe that the public persona of the family was not the private reality of the household. The children were quite well adjusted. I talked with all five children after Stacey's death, and they had no negative feelings or testimony about their father. They all had very high views of both their parents.

In short, in the time I knew Michael Schwartz, I experienced extensive evidence that he was a fantastic father and loyal family man. I experienced no counter indicators to this either in their public life in the church or my time with them in their home.

I should also add that in my profession, I see a lot of people die. Michael died in a very disappointing and painful set of circumstances. However, I have seen only a couple of people die with as much poise and character as he did. This displayed to me a very strong and sincere Christian character that in those few months I came to deeply admire.

One further thing that may be of significance is that I did discuss some end-of-life issues with Michael and Stacey while he was still living. This was precipitated by a disagreement I had with some of Michael's family about when it was appropriate to start preparing for death. Because some of his family was not ready to talk about some of these issues, Michael and Stacey talked with me about them.

My main intention was to encourage Michael to write or video as much as possible for his kids while he was still generally healthy. But Michael and Stacey brought up the issues of putting together a will, its stresses and its content. For whatever purpose it might serve, this is what we discussed in those conversations:

First, keeping all their children together was the highest priority for both of them. This was said and universally presumed in these discussions. Second, they said they had decided the children should go to Michael's sister, Shannon. They did not share with me all the reasons for this, only that Shannon and Sion's very active Christian faith was a significant factor and that both had seen the great benefit of a strong church community on their family. They did not volunteer what their second choice would be, and that was likely because Stacey dying too was the furthest thing from anyone's mind at the time.

Third, let me add that in my opinion these were mutual and permanent decisions for Stacey and Michael. It appeared that Michael's sickness precipitated this making of the will, but did not greatly affect the content of their decisions. I believe the selection of Sion and Shannon as their guardians of choice was as mutual a desire as their absolute desire that their children remain together in a single household. I do not think this was acquiescence on Stacey's part to her dying husband. It appeared to me to be the mutual decision of a strongly united couple.

If I can be of further assistance in any of these matters, please don't hesitate to contact me.

Sincerely,
Rev. Nic Gibson,
MDiv, Associate Pastor
Lynn Haven United Methodist Church

The letter, written by the pastor who was in direct relationship with both Michael and Stacey, brought honor to the deceased couple and dispelled all disgruntled views of what was best for their children. Honor is a gift. It is no coincidence that honor is man's greatest need. Who doesn't like to be honored, including God? When I looked in *Webster's Dictionary*, I saw the word *honor* means "high respect or esteem; to regard with great respect." The Bible clearly shows that there are blessings when we honor others: "My Father will honor the one who serves me" (John 12:26).

One of the challenges we all faced in coming together as one family was the willingness to lay down our lives in both word and deed and honor others before ourselves. This was a daily choice and something we practiced. We couldn't look into the eyes of the children (ours or my brother's) and say this situation of sharing your parents or losing your parents was God's will. But we came to know that God does work all things for our good, as the Bible tells us: "And we know that in all things God works for the good of those who love him, who have been called according to his purpose" (Rom. 8:28). Notice that God places our good before His purpose or will. What an unselfish God, so worthy of honor and glory! This same God laid down His life for us so that we could learn how to honor others in the same way.

While I was taking care of six children, trying to sell our house, and singing on the weekends, Sion was engrossed in his own full-time job at the church and was working with my mother as she prepared the information her attorney would need to present our case in court.

Sion provided his work history as Gateway Church's executive worship pastor, as well as proof of income showing that although I received payment for the time I spent working with the worship team on the weekends, I did not have to work outside the home during the week. And lastly, we had a letter stating that the insurance we carried through the church would be extended to all five of Michael and Stacey's children. From our perspective, we had the means to do what their parents wished. We could provide a home where they could all stay together in a stable environment with a parent at home during the day.

Because both sides of the family had met together and carried on a dialogue about the children, we were already aware of the arguments Stacey's family would likely present to the court. We were confident that the will Michael and Stacey's attorney had prepared at their direction would take precedence over verbal testimony, despite the fact that Stacey had failed to sign the document. However, Mom's attorney continued to meticulously prepare the facts of our case for presentation to the judge.

Sion and I prayed continually about the case. We wanted it to be settled as quickly and peacefully as possible for the sake of the children. With each passing day, we became increasingly more confident that while we were fighting for the spiritual well-being of the children, there was not going to be a battle in the natural. Our sense was that the Lord would go before us and resolve the issue in the best interest of all concerned. After all, there were good people on both sides of the family, and when all was said and done, we would still be connected to each other through our shared love for the children.

A week before the court date, my parents told us to purchase a large passenger van and they would provide the money. At that time I was driving a top of the line Toyota Sienna minivan with leather seats, sunroof, and DVD player with wireless headsets. Basically, it was the closest mommy vehicle to the 350ZX, so I couldn't envision myself in a big white passenger van with big cloth bench seats. This was not exactly an upgrade. I liked to feel my turns, so a top-heavy fifteen-passenger bus was going to be a huge adjustment. "It's ugly, but it's paid for" became our declarative statement as our friends sarcastically made remarks about our new wheels. All six children loved it because there was plenty of room for traveling. Since we didn't have any teenage drivers, this vehicle would become our new "family of ten" transportation. Yeah, baby, we were sporting it! I told Sion, "You know you're a daddy if the only way you can take your family anywhere is by driving a fifteen-passenger van."

Finally, July 15 arrived, and all of the parties appeared before the judge. I'm sure that Michael and Stacey could never have envisioned the level of tension that was present between the two sides of the family that day as we came together seeking a decision about their children.

I had not seen Elizabeth or Emily in four weeks, so all of the children were nervous about how they should respond to one another because of the family feud. Against our wishes, both Elizabeth and Emily were allowed to be present during the ruling.

Both attorneys were well prepared. As expected, the

attorney representing Stacey's family presented a strong argument challenging the legality of a document that did not bear Stacey's signature. He talked about the only life the children had known, which was in Panama City, where all three of their living grandparents and some of their aunts and uncles still resided. He challenged our family's relationship with the children, pointing out that Sion and I lived thirteen hours away and only visited twice each year. He outlined a detailed plan for the children to remain in their own environment, where they would be cared for by several sets of aunts and uncles who were committed to work together in the best interest of the children. All in all it was a compelling argument.

My mom's attorney was equally compelling. He presented all of the documents supporting our willingness and ability to provide a safe and stable home for all five of the children. He drew a sharp contrast between the benefits of the children remaining together as their parents had wished and the potential problems of their being torn apart and raised in separate homes. Supported by my mother's testimony, he established a chronological timeline that began with the diagnosis of Michael's cancer. Next he covered the conversation Sion and I had with Michael and Stacey about becoming their children's guardians and their direction to their attorney regarding their wishes for the children. Finally, he addressed Michael's rapid decline and the hard hit Stacey and the children had taken when he passed away. Clearly, the unending demands of caring for five children took understandable precedence over Stacey's taking time to sign a piece of paper, regardless of its importance. She most certainly did not know that she would also pass away soon.

Mom's attorney stayed on point with the message: Michael and Stacey both went to the attorney. They both agreed to the content of the will naming Shannon and Sion guardians of all five children. Unfortunately, Stacey did not return to seal the document with her signature, but her intent was nonetheless clear.

After seeing the will, the letter written by Michael and Stacey's pastor, and hearing the testimony of others supporting the fact that Michael and Stacey were in agreement about where the children should reside if both of them passed away, the judge ruled in our favor.

Sion and I were awarded full custody of Mary Catherine, Emily, David, and Caroline. We were given temporary custody of fifteen-year-old Elizabeth, who in a few months' time would be allowed to determine for herself whether she wanted to stay with us in Texas or return to Florida.

My mom was given guardianship of the properties. Since the judge determined that she had the greatest vested interest, she was charged with the responsibility of selling the house and also of liquidating any other assets for the well-being of the children.

We did not want to isolate Stacey's side of the family; it was never our intent to do so. We felt it would be good for everyone involved if the children could return to Panama City on a regular basis. The judge also ordered visitation rights allowing the children to go to Florida twice each year to spend time with family and friends.

The atmosphere in the courtroom remained tense despite the fact that the judge had issued his ruling.

While I was thankful that the judge had ruled in our favor, my heart also went out to Stacey's family who were undoubtedly experiencing yet another sense of loss. As I left the courtroom that day walking with Sion, Mom, and Dad, it was all I could do to hold back the tears. Sensing my anguish, Mom took my hand and gently whispered in my ear, "It's going to be OK now. We won."

We won? If this is how it feels to win, then I'd hate to know what it feels like to lose. Both Sion and I knew we had just laid down our own lives to raise five more children when the stamp and signature was placed on the recorded document that day. In honor of Michael and Stacey's will, just as they had wanted, the children would remain together with us in Texas—yet it was going to take an act of our wills to come together as one happy family.

Our prayer was, "God, Your will be done in our lives and in the lives of these children. Let our worship not be something we go and do, but something we live as we honor You by laying down our lives for one another."

God wants us to *honor Him*.

Chapter 6

TRUST HIM

I WRESTLED WITH MY own emotions throughout the thirteen-hour drive back to Texas. My brother's children had just lost both of their parents within a three-year period, and now they were being moved away from those who loved them to a new and unfamiliar environment. The legal proceedings had left a huge fracture between the two sides of their family. Not only did Stacey's mother and siblings have to face the heartbreak of saying good-bye to the children, but also so did my own parents.

"Oh, Lord," I prayed, "please comfort each one of us. Please heal this family. These children have suffered enough." I had no choice but to trust God and leave the matter in His hands; I'd have enough to do once we got home. His Word confronted me when I tried to figure it out on my own: "Trust in the LORD with all your heart and lean not on your own understanding" (Prov. 3:5).

The term Camp Alford took on new meaning once all ten of us were together under one roof. Our home seemed to be shrinking by the day as we struggled those first couple of weeks to adjust to our new living conditions.

It seemed as if Dallas barked all the time. He'd gone from living with five familiar faces to having five new and unfamiliar faces present in his environment. Every little thing would set him off, and with all of the laundry that was now a permanent fixture on the utility room floor, I didn't have the luxury of sending him to what had once been his quiet sanctuary. Camp Alford was a perfect picture of organized chaos—every single day.

Mealtimes were particularly challenging. Everyone wanted to sit down together to eat at night, but it was not possible because we just didn't have enough room at our table. My prayer was that our next house would provide us with a special place where we could come together as a family and actually enjoy eating together.

I knew it was going to take everyone's participation and cooperation for me to run the household. It was already becoming clear that there were those within the family who liked to serve and others who liked to *be* served. Sion and I came up with a weekly chore chart that outlined each child's daily personal tasks, such as making their beds and cleaning their rooms. We also assigned age-appropriate participation in regular household maintenance, including doing laundry, assisting in meal preparation and cleanup, and mowing the yard.

While I was perfecting my skills as camp manager, Sion was busy scouting for houses that would be suitable for our new family. The first thing we did was to create a checklist of the features we needed for a family of ten. In order to make efficient use of our time, we decided that Sion would make the initial review of each potential new home and then narrow the list down to the top three. That's when I would scrutinize each candidate, and together Sion and I would decide which one would work best for our family.

One of the top three houses was a new property that was in the final stages of construction. It just needed to be finished out. The house had an interesting history: although it had never been lived in, it had already had several different potential owners. The builder that started the house decided to stay up north due to the decline of economic growth within his business, and then the financing didn't go through for another couple. So the house sat unfinished and was placed back on the market when we began looking for houses. It seemed as if God had kept this house for us, knowing what we needed and where we needed to be located. Meanwhile we prayed God would lead our steps, and we trusted Him to give us confirmation. When you want direction and clear confirmation on your decision, I encourage you to lean upon His Word and trust Him. The psalmist David wrote in Psalm 119:105, "Your word is a lamp to my feet and a light for my path."

As we walked through the main living areas of the home, I made a mental comparison with the other two homes I'd seen. Any one of the three would've met our basic needs for space. I was just asking God to guide us in our decision when we stepped into the breakfast room and the Realtor explained that it had been expanded in order to accommodate the present owner's oversized table.

The room was absolutely filled with light. Then my eyes gave wonder to the fact that there were exactly *ten* newly installed windows, which happened to be the number of members of our family. Sion and I looked at each other and smiled. Wasn't it just like God to build a brand-new home that would be perfect for our family? And then

He gave us our heart's desire by creating a special place where everyone could feel loved and connected, knowing they each had a place in the family.

Sion and I thought, "Here it is. This will be the place where we have our 'come to Jesus' moments together as a family." We knew without a doubt that this was the place God had prepared for our family, but our dilemma remained the same. In order to buy it, we first had to sell our house that had been on the market for over three years. We had to trust Him.

Since Mary Catherine, David, and Caroline had already been with us for several weeks before Elizabeth and Emily arrived, they were accustomed to the drill we went through each time the house was to be shown to a potential buyer. It was a game to the younger children. Yet with Elizabeth and Mary Catherine being older, it wasn't as much fun for them. The whole routine was more like an annoying disruption.

Another thing Mary Catherine found particularly annoying was the Christian lifestyle that permeated our home. It was only natural for me to refer to the Bible anytime I was giving instruction to my children. I did the same when instructing my nieces and nephew. I usually began by saying, "The Bible says...," and then I'd quote a verse that was appropriate for the circumstance. Mary Catherine enjoyed making fun of my parenting style. "The Bible says? Aunt Shannon, the Bible is something we think about on Sunday. We live the way *we* live the rest of the week."

It was disappointing to hear her talk this way, but it didn't bother me. I understood that although the kids had been involved in their church youth group in Panama

City, their spirits perhaps were not yet reborn because of the trauma they had experienced and the mistrust of God being a good God. Now that they were becoming connected at Gateway Church, I also knew they would have the opportunity to hear the Word of God and to be drawn to Him by the Spirit.

As I mentioned earlier, Sion and I had access to a wonderful group of professional counselors at the church. One of these counselors was an expert on anger management and emotional losses. Since she had the experience we needed, we didn't waste any time in setting an appointment to meet with her. As parents, we wanted to be sensitive to each of our new children's needs. We knew they were grieving, and we wanted to equip ourselves to walk through the process with each of them.

With continued support from our counselor, Sion and I were able to help the children adjust to their new life. Over the next few weeks, they became more settled as each day passed—with the exception of Elizabeth. While the other children were developing new relationships at church, Elizabeth remained isolated. She was still very much connected to her friends in Panama City. And besides, in a few months she would be allowed to decide whether to stay in Texas or return to Florida. There just wasn't much motivation for her to develop relationships here.

The counselor explained that, as the oldest, Elizabeth would experience the most grief. She also reminded us that from the perspective of a young person who'd lost her parents, Elizabeth was preparing to take charge of her life. She told us that this was natural for a girl who'd been through all she'd been through at age fifteen.

As we concluded one particular session with the counselor, she prayed for us and then said, "God will be with you and bless you as you walk through this transition. I want to assure you that in about six months, as Elizabeth and the others begin to develop new relationships, they will put down roots and take ownership of their new lives in Texas."

We had not yet made an offer on the home we'd selected. We didn't want to tie up our money in a down payment without having a contract on our house. We knew there was a possibility that someone else could make an offer and we'd lose the house, but there was just nothing we could do until we had a buyer. So many things needed to happen, and they needed to happen quickly. School would be starting soon, and we didn't want to have to reenroll the children in Mansfield schools, only to be uprooted in a few weeks or months to move to another school district. Sion and I made a conscious decision to take life one day at a time and to trust God for the miracles we needed.

July 29 started off like every other weekday. Sion gave me a kiss as he left for his one-hour commute to the church. I turned my attention to the kitchen since the kids were waking up and would soon be coming in for breakfast.

For some reason, it was as if they all came completely unglued at once that morning in the kitchen. Everyone was complaining, arguing, and venting their frustrations. After weeks of being piled on top of each other, we'd all had it—including me. But I knew I didn't have the luxury of throwing a pity party for myself. The boys were now crammed into one room. My oldest son, Si, was sleeping on a mattress on the floor because he had outgrown his bunk beds where the little boys were sleeping. In an effort to give everyone their own bed, I had four girls, ages fifteen, fourteen, eleven, and five, sleeping in two bunk beds in the same room with Brooke adjacent to them in her own bed. Five girls were sharing the same bathroom. Let's just say that is way too many bottoms using the same space. At night I would individually take Caroline and David to our shower downstairs so that we were more spread out throughout the house. I think Sion would drive slower on his way home than he did to work.

Reminding myself that I was the grown-up in the house, I quickly pulled myself together and addressed the group. "Look, guys, I know it's hard; it's difficult for everybody. But we are going to have to learn how to work together and how to love each other despite our differences. Doing this is going to be a process. It will take time. But the goal today is to move from where we are now to closer to the place we want to be."

Whether one is managing employees, volunteers, or a family, it is imperative to continually speak the vision and reiterate what it will take to get where you're going. That is exactly what I was doing. "We're going to have to pull together," I told them. Then to break the tension I added, "And that includes the dog!"

That's when I glanced at my watch and noticed the time and date. It was ten o'clock on July 29—Michael's birthday. That gave me an idea.

"Kids, today is Michael's birthday, and I don't think he'd be happy with the way we've all behaved today. He was a fun person, a happy person who enjoyed helping other people. If he could look over the sapphire seal of heaven at us right now, I think he'd have a different kind of day in mind for us."

I could see the change in their faces as they all began to smile. "Let's make this a fun, festive day and not get on each other's nerves. Let's be kind and considerate of each other in honor of your father and uncle. Let's go back to what we know. Let's get our chores done and then have a fun day."

Steve Martin's grandmother in the movie *Cheaper by the Dozen* had invented the game "apple smear" as a great way for the children to laugh and enjoy the family. At the Alford camp we had soda can shake 'em up wars. Let me explain. It was every man for himself as each person ran for his life shaking a can of soda. At just the right time you pop the top and unload on a running and screaming sibling target. This source of entertainment only gets better when followed by ketchup pack fights as the lawn sprinklers are randomly set to come on in different stations every ten minutes. This was the only way to entertain kids outside in 100-degree weather with no community pool.

At two o'clock that afternoon I'd just returned from the grocery store when the Realtor called and said a couple wanted to see the house as soon as possible. "OK, kids, it's show time," I said. "Put the mattresses up and pick up the Legos. Let's be ready to leave in one hour." It was a mad, fire-alarm rush of getting the house cleaned so that we could leave, but we made it out the door in just a little under an hour with dog and cage in hand. We had this down to an art.

Usually the showings lasted fifteen to twenty minutes, but this one took longer. I kept returning to the house to see if it was clear, but each time I drove by, they were still there. One of the kids said, "Maybe they like it." After nearly an hour they left, and we were glad to get back to playing and doing laundry.

When Sion got home that evening and asked about my day, I said, "Someone came to see the house today, and they stayed a long time." Neither one of us thought any more about it until the Realtor called about eight o'clock that night.

"The couple who saw the house this afternoon is very interested and wants a second showing." They had asked some specific questions about the house, which Sion and I answered. Before we ended the conversation with the Realtor, we'd set up a time for the second showing on the following day. And within a week's time we had a contract on the house.

The offer we made on the new construction house with ten windows was accepted. Although we wouldn't be in our new home until well after the kids had started school, we were glad that the three-year real estate roller-coaster ride was about to come to an end.

Sion and I now had a completely new perspective where the house was concerned. Had we sold our home three years ago when we first put it on the market, we would be living closer to the church by now. But we still wouldn't have enough space for our rapidly expanding family. God knew even then what our needs were going to be, and we now believed that what we'd experienced with the house was His grace in action. We realized that

He'd not been keeping our new house *from* us. He'd been keeping it *for* us.

Psalm 84:11 says, "For the Lord God is a sun and shield; the Lord bestows favor and honor; no good thing does he withhold from those whose walk is blameless." This scripture has always been one of my favorite refrigerator verses because of its declaration of faith in the midst of war and turmoil.

Many times in our lives we have seen God be gracious and good to us when we walk in humility and are clothed in His righteousness. God has been both light and protection, and as painful as some situations have been to walk through, God has been so faithful. We have learned that when we submit our lives daily to Him as an act of worship, He illuminates our path, protects our future, and gives peace to our hearts as we sing, "I will trust You, God. I will trust in You."

Registering eight children with two last names in three different schools was quite an adventure. In order to register the kids, the Trophy Club School District required that we provide documentation confirming that we were selling our house in Mansfield and moving to Trophy Club. Next I had to check health immunization records and schedule appointments for physicals for those who wanted to participate in sports. Mary Catherine had a heart murmur and was required to go to a specialist before entering the water for the swim team. David, who was painfully thin and was always the last person left at the table, was vitamin D deficient. Elizabeth said after their dad died, David rarely ate a full meal, but now his appetite was growing.

In a matter of weeks everyone's immunization records were up-to-date and Mary Catherine's doctor had given her permission to swim. The three-week process had gone surprisingly well, and soon all eight children were looking forward to sharing a new adventure together.

Although we knew Elizabeth might not be with us permanently, we were delighted when she decided to join her new school's color guard. This meant she would now get to meet other kids her age who shared similar interests. I was more excited than she was that first day I drove her to practice. We were already running a few minutes late, but when I pulled up to the curb to let her out, she didn't want to leave the van.

Realizing that she was dealing with a lot of new and unfamiliar situations in her life, I reminded her that all of her siblings and cousins were sharing the same experience of being a new student this school year. I assured her she was going to like this school, and she would love being on the color guard here as much as she loved it in Florida. Elizabeth still wasn't convinced. I sent up a silent prayer saying, "Lord, I need some help here. Please show me what to do to help her."

At that precise moment a Suburban pulled to the curb just ahead of me. I recognized the driver as a woman named Catherine, a member of the Gateway Choir. Her daughter was on the school's color guard. "Thank You, Lord," I said as I left my vehicle to go speak to Catherine. We introduced the girls to each other, and the two of them headed off to practice together.

I couldn't wait to call Sion and tell him what had

just happened. Here I'd been upset, thinking Elizabeth was going to be late to her very first practice, and God arranged things in a way that she didn't have to go alone. I never cease to be amazed at His perfect timing. The psalmist wrote, "I will say of the Lord, 'He is my refuge and my fortress, my God, in whom I trust'" (Ps. 91:2). You can trust Him.

Once school started, Camp Alford's highway 360 travels and often known parking lot road service sprung to life again. I was the first to awaken in the morning to ensure that the first group of kids, who had to be at school at seven thirty, got dressed and were ready to leave the house no later than six thirty for the one-hour drive. Sion made sure that the other children were dressed and ready to leave with him at seven thirty. After dropping them at their respective schools by eight thirty, he had just enough time to make it to work by nine o'clock.

Each day when I returned from my two-hour round trip, I started my new routine of packing the house while still doing the shopping, cooking, and laundry. I would leave the house at one fifty to pick up all three elementary children by two fifty. Sion would pick up Brooke at the middle school by four o'clock, followed by the three in high school by four fifteen. He would then fight his way through traffic to make it home by five thirty for supper. This gave me enough time to help the elementary children finish their homework and then have supper ready by the time they all walked in the door.

Suppertime was usually loud. We came up with the "raise your hand if you have something to share about your day" rule so that no two people were interrupting each other. After supper was definitely the most stressful time of the day as the "clearing the table, washing dishes, dealing with drama, bathing, and putting kids to bed" ritual happened five days a week. Oftentimes Sion and I would blow kisses to each other across the room and wish it were nine o'clock. That's when lights were out and the kids were either in their beds sleeping or preparing themselves for the next day.

By then the chore schedule was in full motion. The children helped with dishes, folding and putting away laundry, taking out the trash, making beds, and mowing the lawn. In addition to our hectic weekday schedules, Sion and I were still participating in multiple worship services on the weekend. I had a mental image of our individual lives portrayed as a group of colorful carnival rides. Each one was simultaneously spinning and whirling, fueled by a color-coded travel schedule. I was thankful for all God had done in our lives, but I couldn't wait for the day when we could leave the carnival.

We moved into our new home at the end of September 2009. It was wonderful to have enough bedrooms and bathrooms to comfortably accommodate everyone. Sion's commute to work had been cut from one hour to only fifteen minutes, and we were now only half a mile from the kids' schools. But perhaps the most significant change for me was the fact that now all of us could come together around our new dining table and enjoy a meal as a family. At our home in Mansfield, we had to take turns sitting at the table or the kitchen counter, rotating our nine chairs. Invariably someone was left to eat while standing every night, and it usually ended up being me. So I hung a large cross in a prominent location before entering the breakfast room in our new home. Each day as I passed by it, I prayed, "Lord, thank You for our new home."

That six-week period of time when we were driving back and forth was a difficult journey. We look back now and can't believe we were able to do it, but by the grace of God we endured. I learned firsthand that when the road is too hard for you to bear, that is when He steps in and you move over.

In his letter to the Corinthians the apostle Paul wrote the following: "All praise to God, the Father of our Lord Jesus Christ. God is our merciful Father and the source of all comfort. He comforts us in all our troubles so that we can comfort others. When they are troubled, we will be able to give them the same comfort God has given us" (2 Cor. 1:3–4, NLT).

You can trust Him.

Just as our counselor had said, the children began establishing new relationships and putting down roots. This was not only true for my brother's children, but for my kids as well, since they'd all started the year at new schools. We were particularly pleased to see that Elizabeth was becoming more accepting of her circumstances, which we attributed to her involvement with her school's color guard. She and Brittany, the girl she met the first day of practice, had become best friends; they both attended the same youth group and were involved at Gateway Church together.

Things were going great as some old situations were dissolving, but new issues began to surface. As we would come to understand later, it is not uncommon for children who have lost their parents to develop an entitlement mentality. Oftentimes this attitude begins when they experience the initial outpouring of love and support from immediate family members and friends, followed by the understanding support of their church, school, and community.

An attitude of entitlement says, "Because I've gone through this terrible situation, I'm entitled to be given to." Although we didn't recognize it at the time, Sion and I saw this attitude in several of the children soon after they arrived at our house. I playfully gave Emily the nickname of Violet, the little girl in the movie *Willie Wonka and the Chocolate Factory* whose mantra was "I want it, and I want it now!"

I constantly had to remind her that she was not the only child in the house and assured her she would be taken care of when it was her turn. I would say, "Kids, we all have to lay down our lives and honor one another above ourselves. We all have to share. We are going through a process of change, and it requires that we die to ourselves." I knew this was a particularly difficult concept for the younger children to grasp, but it was true nonetheless.

While Michael's children were feeling as if they were entitled to certain benefits because of all the bad things that had happened to them, our children were having their own issues. Si, Brooke, and Austin were experiencing their own sense of loss in that the relationship they'd had with Sion and me was forever changed. It was frustrating for them to no longer have access to the quality time with us they'd once had. Thankfully, Sion and I had a wealth of support resources available to us through Gateway Church, and we took time for regular "come to Jesus" meetings at our breakfast table to share how we felt about the changes and how we were going to allow these changes to make us better and not bitter. Through honoring one another's feelings, we were able to address a selfish mentality, or the feeling of entitlement, and allow time for change through the washing of His Word.

The October date on which Elizabeth was to make her decision about where she wanted to live was approaching. She had once been adamant about returning to Florida, but now she was undecided. She talked regularly to her relatives in Panama City who assured her that if she decided to return, she would be welcome to live with them so that she could finish high school where she had started. I explained to her that although returning to Florida might be the easiest decision for her, she should consider the effect it would have on her siblings.

I assured her that if she chose to stay with us, she would get to be a normal fifteen-year-old without having the responsibility of being a mother to her three sisters and her brother. That was my job. Her presence would give them the security of having their older sister with them, and when the time came for her to go to college, the separation would be a natural one. Sion and I did not want to pressure Elizabeth into choosing to stay. Instead, we wanted to give her enough pertinent information to enable her to make an informed decision. The rest would be up to her.

On the day our court-appointed guardianship of Elizabeth expired, she was still undecided about what she wanted to do. Although she was living with us in Texas, she was technically a ward of the State of Florida. Missing the deadline for filing Elizabeth's response created some legal red tape that had to be addressed, which the attorney was handling. But the bigger question was, when would Elizabeth make her decision? As it turned out, we only had to wait a few weeks.

The children would be making their first visit to Panama City in November. Stacey's older sister and her husband would make the drive to Texas and then return with the kids to Florida for the week of Thanksgiving. On the evening they arrived to pick up the kids, I'd assumed they would spend the night and leave the following morning. I was horrified when I learned they intended to return immediately.

I didn't rest well at all that night. I spent a lot of time praying for Stacey's sister and her husband as they made the second of two thirteen-hour drives that day. And when I wasn't praying for them, I was thinking about Elizabeth. Would the door of her heart be closed to the life she'd known in Panama City, or would she feel as if she'd just come home? Would she even return to Texas after Thanksgiving? I had to trust God.

I was relieved the next morning when I got the call telling me that everyone had arrived safe and sound. The children were staying at several different homes, and I knew they would have a great time reconnecting with their family and friends that week.

In the meantime Si, Brooke, and Austin loved having Mom and Dad to themselves. Sion and I were also enjoying the holiday break, although the unsettled issue regarding Elizabeth's decision still weighed heavy on our hearts. Our prayer was, "Lord, we've done literally everything You've asked us to do and everything that can be done. It is now totally in Your hands; Your will be done."

The day had come for them to return to Texas, and to our delightful surprise Elizabeth did indeed return with her sisters and brother following their Thanksgiving in Florida. When the noisy group of siblings burst through the front door that night, she went straight to her room to deposit her things without greeting us. Pretty soon she came back downstairs to say good-bye to her aunt and uncle.

Sion and I were in the living room when an unusually serious Elizabeth approached us. Without a word of hello she got straight to the point. "I'm ready to sign the paper making you my permanent guardians."

Sion and I could never have imagined the impact her decision would have on our entire family. Without the weight of indecision burdening her fifteen-year-old heart, Elizabeth was a different person. Her entire countenance and demeanor confirmed the freedom her spirit was experiencing. Once Mary Catherine, Emily, David, and Caroline saw their sister was happy and knew she had chosen to remain with them, they were happy too. I thanked God for everything He had done to bring us to this place. It was amazing what all had been accomplished in only the last six months of the year. But the year wasn't over yet.

We took our first Christmas card photo the next day and captured the happy hearts of two families becoming one. Then one month later, during a special time of worship at our Christmas musical *The Scrooge*, I openly wept as I watched Elizabeth, Mary Catherine, Emily, David, and little Caroline go forward and give their lives to Jesus.

God had just answered the prayer I'd prayed only weeks earlier as I stood in front of the cross on the wall of our home and gave Him Elizabeth. Many times Sion and I had told her we were not letting go of her because she was worth fighting for and we loved her. Our family was now one in the Lord. God had proven His Word to be true. "Come to me, all you who are weary and burdened, and I will give you rest. Take my yoke upon you and learn from me, for I am gentle and humble in heart, and you will find rest for your souls. For my yoke is easy and my burden is light" (Matt. 11:28–30).

We can *trust Him*.

PS: My brother's children had their first white Christmas that year, which was also an answer to prayer since they had never seen snow.

Chapter 7

FOLLOW HIM

AS YOU CAN already imagine, I quickly discovered that planning and preparing meals for a family of ten was often both costly and time-consuming. Although I was using my Crock-Pot often, I couldn't just add more water to a recipe to make it work for ten people. So I didn't waste any time in developing an effective shopping strategy utilizing only three key components: Walmart, Costco, and a legal-size, yellow note pad. Yes, I know...my daughter, Brooke, told me there was an app for grocery shopping, but I'm old school.

I began by drawing a vertical line down the middle of the page. On the right side of the page I made a column listing the days of the week. On the left side I listed the ingredients for each night's supper. Breakfast and lunch menus were so rudimentary that I had them memorized. Cereal and waffles were the morning staples for our youth group, along with scrambled eggs and health shakes for the athletes. Four of the kids liked to buy their lunch at school, and four preferred to take their lunches, so making lunch purchases was predictable and easy.

One day as I was placing six gallons of milk beneath my already overfilled cart, another shopper stopped and said, "Oh my goodness, how many times a month do you have to do this?"

"I do this every week," I told her.

"What in the world...how many people are you feeding?"

"Well, I have eight children, plus my husband and me."

The woman's mouth dropped open as she shook her head and gave me a quick look from head to toe. "Honey, you don't look like you have more than one or two children at the most." Then she took a step back, closed her eyes, raised her hands, and declared, "The Lord bless you and keep you!"

I added a hearty amen, and we both had a good laugh that day. I've since gotten used to the strange looks I get from people when they see me pushing a cart so full that it looks like it might explode. I'm such a regular at the two stores that I could probably be on a commercial for them.

Our family had literally doubled in size, and I pondered, "I stopped at three children because I felt I was outnumbered. Now I have an endless amount of 'noise makers' at my house."

As predicted, it didn't take long for "8 Is Enough" to develop friendships with others. When one of the children would ask, "Can I invite a friend to youth group?" Sion and I would jokingly respond, "We *are* a youth group!" We used our big white van to drive our children and many others back and forth to youth events, and, oh, what a wonderful day it was when we finally had another driver in the family.

When my brother's children first moved from Florida to Texas, his oldest daughter, Elizabeth, already had her driver's permit. Like any almost-sixteen-year-old she was looking forward to getting her license. But I don't think she was looking forward to it half as much as I was. The very thought of having another driver in the house to help with the demands of running everybody to and fro or to pick up last minute groceries gave me reason to rejoice. It also pleased me to know that Elizabeth was attentive and responsible in everything she set her hand to.

Throughout the months we'd spent teaching the kids about responsibility, we had talked with the older children about the time when they would each begin driving. Just as in every other area of their lives, they would have standards. They would be responsible for cleaning any family vehicle they drove. When the time came that they had a vehicle of their own, they would be responsible for assisting financially with the gas, maintenance, and insurance.

As it turned out, my grandmother would be turning ninety in the same month that Elizabeth turned sixteen. Although Mimi enjoyed her independence, driving had become more difficult for her since she'd had some extensive surgery on her shoulder. Both Mom and Mimi felt that it was time for her to stop driving, and she was only too happy to give her 2003 Chevy Impala (with only 23,000 miles on it) to Elizabeth.

Since Elizabeth would be the first child to obtain a license, I was not familiar with the process or requirements in our state. After Sion did some research, we decided to forgo the traditional driver's education program and take the more economical online route. Elizabeth completed all of her studies, and after downloading the required forms, I took her to our local Texas driver's license office.

The woman at the counter greeted us and looked over all of the paperwork to make sure it was in order. But when she saw Elizabeth's Florida driver's permit, her countenance changed. "I'm so sorry, but you're going to have to wait a whole year before you can obtain a Texas license. Our law requires that you have one year of driver education."

Fighting back tears, Elizabeth said, "You've got to be kidding. I've completed all of the required paperwork, I've already been driving, and now I've got to wait?"

I felt terrible for her. Had we known that a year of driver education was required for new student drivers in Texas, I could have taken her to Florida to obtain her license, then return to Texas and just change her residency. As the saying goes, "Hindsight is twenty-twenty." But that had nothing to do with the situation at hand.

"Look," I explained to the woman behind the counter, "I have eight children, and I *have* to have another driver. My husband works during the day, and I need someone to help me get the kids to school and where they need to be. Can't anything be done?"

The clerk explained that the state offered something called a hardship license for minors, which was granted for only four reasons:

1. The applicant's family faces unusual economic hardship and is being deprived of the basic necessities of life.
2. The applicant has an ill family member who needs transportation to medical

treatment, or the applicant must drive in her place to keep the household running.

3. The applicant is enrolled in a vocational educational program.
4. An immediate family member has died, and remaining family members need him/her to drive temporarily to carry on household routines.

We applied immediately for the hardship license. Although it took almost six months to complete that process, the entire family celebrated on the day that Elizabeth received not only her Texas driver's license but also permanent custody of Mimi's car keys.

Si was the next one to obtain his license, and by then we knew the ropes. Sion set him up online to complete his driver's education course, and he was parent-taught the rest. When Sion took him to get his license, he had already completed his requirements and had no problem in passing the test.

Today we have four children who are driving: Elizabeth, Si, Mary Catherine, and Brooke. In each instance God honored their hard work, and we were able to provide them with a vehicle.

It has been a tremendous blessing to our family to have these vehicles. Our driveway is always full, and it requires a lot of organization each night before bedtime to determine how to arrange the vehicles according to who leaves first the next morning. It looks like we have company all the time, but we say, "We *are* company!"

There is never a dull moment at our house. During the

summer Si plays baseball all over the Dallas-Fort Worth metroplex; he also plays for the high school team during school. He mows the lawn, details cars, umpires Little League games, and works at various sports camps for elementary-age kids. Mary Catherine swims throughout the year, teaches swimming lessons, and is a lifeguard at the community pool. Elizabeth, now off at college, comes home on weekends and helps lead worship in kids' church while Brooke babysits and is a cheerleader for the high school. All four assist in the maintenance of their vehicles, while consistently maintaining good grades in school. Yes, I am a proud mommy. These kids are not perfect, but they have chosen to follow Him.

One day as I was having a rare quiet moment at home, my attention was drawn to the large cross hanging on the wall. As I contemplated the sacrifice that Jesus had made for each one of us when He willingly submitted to the most heinous death imaginable, I felt the Lord speak to me: "I want you to purchase ten small crosses and add them to the wall with the large existing one. Each cross will represent the individual life of each person in this household." The crosses would be placed underneath His and would serve as a reminder that we are all under His authority, and that in order to be successful as we transition into one family, each person must be willing to pick up their own cross and follow Him.

I did what the Lord had instructed me to do.

Several days later we were enjoying a family game night with the four younger children while the older ones were at a youth group event. Caroline, having the luck of the Irish (with my helping her make the right moves), was winning at what we call the "Not So Nice" board game. We told the children this would be the last hand before it was time to brush their teeth and go to bed. Each person took a turn. Then, when David made his last move, it caused Caroline to lose her spot, and the game was over. Caroline buried her head in the pillow.

As we asked questions about what had happened, everyone threw in their cards and made their own remarks. Sion quieted everyone and said, "Let's pray, brush your teeth, and go get in bed."

Caroline leaned over to me and confessed, "I can't pray. I cheated. That's why I lost. If I would have moved the exact number I had rolled, David wouldn't have hit me, causing me to go back to the starting point."

"Caroline, I'm so proud of you for telling the truth," I said.

Then she said, "I looked at my cross on the wall in front of me, and I knew I couldn't pray until I confessed the truth."

We all piled up on Caroline and hugged her. I was glad I had obeyed the Lord and that she was willing to follow Him.

Sion and I knew we had to establish structure within the home in order for the ten of us to be able to function on all levels. Our greatest desire, but most challenging feat, was laying down the steps for the kids to follow after God. We knew we couldn't make them love God, but it was still going to be our responsibility to bring them to an understanding of what it meant to love Him and how to follow Him. In John 21:15–19, Jesus made it very plain when He asked Peter, "Do you love Me?" When Peter answered yes, Jesus said, "Then tend My lambs, feed My sheep, and follow Me." Our first step as the parents of eight children was tending lambs.

It was important from the beginning that we treated all of them with a sense of fairness. From the oldest to the youngest, we wanted them to know that they were equally loved, equally cared for, and equally provided for. While we were careful to monitor what the younger children were watching on TV, some of the older kids thought that they should have their own say about what they watched. We had to explain that just because they were older didn't mean they could watch anything they wanted. We taught them that as they matured and began making their own choices, they must at all times be responsible to guard their hearts. As the Bible says, "Above all else, guard your heart, for it is the wellspring of life" (Prov. 4:23). Until they were on their own, we would be there to guide them. Mary Catherine loved watching MTV and other late night shows that we didn't allow our children to watch. When I would tell her to please change the channel and watch something else, she would mimic me saying, "The Bible says," as I would go through the repetitive ritual of sharing a scripture.

Although I knew she loved me and was glad I cared enough to watch over her and her siblings, we would butt heads over this issue. Unfortunately she wasn't the only one who would argue, roll eyes, or talk back. So I would continue my lectures by saying, "Girls, that's rude and disrespectful," and then they would fall back in the pillows and giggle. By that point I would know the lesson was over, and I would pray, "God, let something I say eventually sink in."

In the past, David and Caroline had watched things

on TV that had opened the doors for them to be frightened. So for months they had to have a light on in order to sleep, or else they didn't feel safe. This, of course, was annoying to their roommates who were no longer afraid of the "boogie man." As much as we reassured them they were safe, it took months for them to settle in for the night and sleep. The first scripture we shared was, "For God has not given us a spirit of fear, but of power and of love and of a sound mind" (2 Tim. 1:7, NKJV). They had experienced death three times in their immediate family, so shutting their eyes at night and not knowing what tomorrow would bring was already frightening. Adding scary movies about monsters and death didn't help.

In order for my young "little people" to grasp what this verse meant, I broke it down and explained, "There will be many times in your life when the spirit of fear will come knocking at your door, but God has given you something stronger and bigger on the inside. We have His love, His power, and His sound mind. So when you feel afraid, you tell that boogie man, 'Go! Get out of here!'"

Since Caroline had the most vivid imagination when she was describing something or sharing a story, I knew she would need something that she could reenact. This suggestion seemed to help her, but I'll never forget the look she gave me when I told her the tooth fairy was going to visit her after she lost her first tooth.

For weeks she had been babying a loose tooth. Every time she talked, it would wiggle, move crooked, and dangle in the breeze, so when she showed me the dangling tooth, I was so excited. "Caroline, it's your first loose tooth!" All the girls where clamoring around her, excited for this "big girl" moment. I almost had her convinced that I could painlessly remove it free of charge, but she would not fall for any of my smooth-talking dental lingo. Now, finally, her time had come, and she proudly presented the tooth to me in her hand. She was so excited because what five-year-old doesn't look forward to a visitation from the tooth fairy? Especially when you have seen your other siblings reap the benefits for years before you. At least that is what I thought.

It was bedtime, so we walked upstairs and she brushed her teeth as we talked about what she needed to do with the tooth. "What exactly is going to happen with my tooth?" she asked.

I said, "Well, first let's place the 'tooth fairy stop here sign' in the window, and I'll help you jump up into the top bunk bed." Then I said, "OK, you place the tooth in this bag and put it under your pillow. Sometime in the night the tooth fairy will come and take your tooth and give you a prize."

She giggled and grinned and then we prayed. I went to turn out the light, and she jumped up and said, "Wait, come here!" She grabbed my arm and said, "What does this tooth fairy look like?" By this point she wanted nothing to do with something flying in the window. Prize or no prize, it didn't matter. It took me ten minutes to convince her to let go of me and lie back down. I told her there was nothing to be afraid of and that the tooth fairy was very sweet.

She still was not persuaded this was going to be an enjoyable experience, so I finally had to tell her, "Caroline, the tooth fairy is me! I'm going to come into your room and reach under the pillow, take the tooth, and leave you a prize."

"Oh!" she gasped. Then she let go of me and told me good night. We both laughed, and she was delighted the next morning that she'd slept right through the tooth fairy's visitation.

Going back to John 21:15–19, in keeping with how to lead the children to a deeper love for God, we saw that step number two was "feed my sheep." Sion was continually bringing home books and sharing related materials that would encourage our big kids to be a light and witness, to follow God and not their peers. Although I knew it was important to teach them how to follow Him, I needed to relax and enjoy building relationships with all of my girls even if we didn't agree on everything.

As I mentioned before, Mary Catherine was accustomed to staying up late and watching TV or movies with her mom. She shared this special memory with me one night while I was fussing at her about what she was watching. I decided we needed a regular girls' movie night. On Sunday night we planned to meet on the couch and pile up like puppies to watch something together. This helped our relationship grow because I found out later, after the children had taken the Five Love Languages test by Gary Chapman, that quality time and receiving gifts were her love languages (as well as all the other girls').

Another issue that caused headaches and strife was that the younger children didn't understand why they could not stay up as late as the older kids. We had a particularly challenging time establishing a consistent bedtime for all four of the youngest "little people." I can only imagine how difficult it had been for Stacey to maintain a household on her own while working full-time. It took the help of family members and friends to ensure that kids got to school and activities on time. Not surprisingly, there were no set bedtimes or processes before the kids went to sleep at night. As a single mom, Stacey focused on daily survival.

Both Emily and David were accustomed to staying up as late as a teenager would, and the results of this unhealthy pattern had been all too apparent during school hours. They were inattentive in class and didn't function well. While they were living in Panama City, their doctor prescribed medication to help keep them alert and focused. But it was clear to us that their bodies were suffering from a lack of rest and discipline. Breaking this pattern did not happen without a struggle, but in a few months' time we saw a marked change in their behavior and attitude.

While everyone else was making As and Bs in school, Emily and David struggled—not because they weren't as smart as the others but because they had just bought the lie that they couldn't do their schoolwork. They would say it was too hard when the reality was, they had developed a lazy pattern and were able to manipulate others to help them do the work for them.

Sion and I knew that if we were going to be successful in helping them achieve all they were capable of in school, we first had to get to the root of this false belief. We found out that the problem started when they'd lost their father and only escalated after their mother had passed away. In the community where they lived in Florida, everyone knew their situation. Out of compassion teachers often excused their incomplete assignments, saying, "OK, I knew your dad," or "I knew your mom, and I'm so sorry for your loss." Emily and David had even been able to get out of some classes altogether.

The children also experienced more privileges than their classmates. The natural desire to help those in need caused their teachers and many people in the community to give to them constantly. The generosity of others can be a tremendous blessing in a time of need. This same generosity can also cause the one being blessed to believe that he or she is entitled to special treatment and to think, "I should be the first in line because of my situation," or "I don't have to finish this project because I'm feeling sad."

When we moved them from Florida to Texas schools, Sion and I were careful to set the same standards for my brother's children as we'd set for our own. "Guys, there's no reason why everybody can't make As and Bs. The score you need to earn a B is now an eighty, so you've got twenty points to work within. Every one of you is capable of that."

Despite our encouragement and support, the kids continued to struggle in school. They leaned on those old habits and patterns of being excused, which were causing them not to develop, not to grow, and not to persevere. Sion and I felt as if we were in a battle for the kids' future, but we just didn't know who—or what—we were battling until we heard a message at church one weekend from Jimmy Evans.

In addition to being one of the elders at Gateway Church, Jimmy Evans is a best-selling author. He and his wife, Karen, are the hosts of *Marriage Today,* a television broadcast aimed at strengthening marriages and families. Jimmy's message that day pertained to people who had suffered great tragedies in life. He explained that oftentimes individuals walk away from devastating circumstances with a mentality that says, "Because this thing has happened to me, now God owes me."

He went on to say that God does not respond to a prayer that demands, "God, You owe me! Now what are You going to give me?" God responds to our faith. When we approach God with a "You owe me" mentality, we are not approaching Him as our Father. In essence, we have therefore developed an *orphan mentality.*

Sion and I couldn't believe what we were hearing. We looked at each other, and then we looked at the children who were there with us. I could tell by their expressions that we were all thinking the same thing: this man must have been listening to some of our conversations at home.

At last Sion and I knew what it was we were dealing with. We didn't waste any time calling a family meeting the minute we got home. Seated at our special table, we had a roundtable discussion with our group that night.

"Look, there are some heart issues and some attitudes here," I said. "It's not something we're just addressing in the five of my brother's children. It's something that is a common thread in this family. I've seen it in all of us around the table. We've each said these things and had these feelings at some point in our lives. It's a heart issue. What are we going to do to change our mind-set? How are we going to resist those feelings and not allow this mentality to control us and dictate who we are and where we're going?"

As our family prayed together that night, Sion and I knew that we'd turned a corner. Everyone in the family was now aware of the orphan mentality. That competitive, manipulative mind-set would no longer be swept under the rug but would instead be pulled onto the carpet to be dealt with on the spot. Now the unnecessary name-calling and "baby fighting" from the orphan mentality that had wreaked such havoc in our lives was coming to an end. We decided then and there it would no longer be allowed to control our thoughts and actions. The orphan mentality had just been evicted from our home.

Rather than blaming the lack of discipline or laziness on the effects of an orphan mentality, Sion and I decided we would focus on the positive aspect of building character in the children. We made each child accountable for his or her grades, regardless of their age.

We believed that teaching accountability at the elementary school level would produce the character the children needed to succeed throughout their educational years. If they learned how to organize and care for their things at the elementary level, they would already have a set routine when they reached middle school and began having multiple classes. Then, when grades really mattered as they were making preparation for higher education, the principles would already be instilled. Rather than having an "I can't" mentality, the children would be able to say with confidence, "OK, I know I can do this."

We began Bible memorization with those who struggled in order to combat the strongholds that had developed. Here are few of those scriptures that helped our group:

> I can do all things through Christ who strengthens me.
>
> —Philippians 4:13, nkjv

> Intelligent children make their parents proud; lazy students embarrass their parents.
>
> —Proverbs 15:20, The Message

> Lazy people want much but get little, but those who work hard will prosper.
>
> —Proverbs 13:4, nlt

Getting the kids to accept this new mentality happened one step at time. As I mentioned before, several had come to rely heavily on either getting help with projects or having them dismissed altogether. In addition to encouraging the children that they could complete their assignments, we also offered incentives for reaching their goals.

Once set, we let them know the privilege they would earn when they reached a goal. All along the path of achievement, they knew exactly what was expected of them. If they failed to reach a goal, they knew it wasn't the end of the line. Rather, it would just take a little longer to get what they wanted.

"It's all up to you," I told them. "You're the only one in this race, and we're the cheerleaders helping you along the way. I can't be there in the classroom with you, but I can be a parent, and I can help you study. It's your responsibility to complete your assignments in class and then listen to the teacher and write down what you need to do at home. If the teacher tells me you're not completing assignments, then you'll not be allowed to take recess at school, and there will be no TV or games when you get home. So when it's time to be at school, it's time to work—it's time to take care of those responsibilities and be diligent about it."

I knew that transitioning from old habits and lack of structure to a new set of standards and rules was going to be a challenge for my brother's kids. I also knew there was more at stake than their grades. Not only had we just taken them out of their school and a situation where people catered to them because of their situation, we were literally taking them out of an environment that was leading them to a fruitless life filled with nothing but excuses.

In the course of our breaking the orphan mentality and its accompanying excuses, we also discovered another issue that had to be dealt with. Oftentimes, when one of the kids would fail to complete an assignment or would get a bad grade, the others would single out that child for ridicule.

"Look at who didn't finish their work."

"You can't do anything right."

"You're stupid."

This is what we call "baby fighting." Baby fighters are insecure people who look for ways to tear others down so that they can appear superior, or above someone else. But as a child of God, our security comes from knowing who we are in Christ, not from our abilities or what we think we can do. A baby fighter is stopped in his or her prideful tracks when they realize that apart from Him, they can do nothing. (See John 15:5.)

At their ages they had no way of knowing how harmful words can be, especially for the younger children. This was a practice that Sion and I had to bring to a stop. We addressed the situation by explaining that the only reason people cut down others is because they are insecure about themselves. As we reiterated this truth on a consistent basis, it caused the older kids to look inside themselves and discover why they were lashing out. Once they had rid themselves of their own insecurities, they were able to change the way they interacted with their siblings. As a result, they all began feeling more confident and capable, believing that they could succeed.

One thing Sion and I are adamant about is not putting up with any one viciously tearing down someone else. A family should be a place where we learn and grow in the knowledge of how to love and serve one another by honoring each other above ourselves. Good communication and showing honor is imperative to developing long-lasting relationships. Yes, we like to joke around, but without a good relationship, the jokes can be destructive. We are firm on "nipping in the bud" such behavior, and we show no tolerance for a mean heart. Why? Because when we allow those we have direct authority over to speak cutting, derogative remarks to others, strongholds are built not only in the recipient but also in the giver, thus hindering their views of God and their ability to follow Him.

In 1 Thessalonians 5:11 we read, "Therefore encourage one another and build each other up." This is a staple verse around our home. Day by day, we are building into our children the Christlike character that will enable them to stand and oppose all the schemes the enemy may bring against them. When anyone says, "I just can't do this; it's too hard," we say, "You *can* do it. You are capable. You are smart."

In dealing with the orphan mentality, one thing we wanted to make sure across the board with all of our kids was that we were not going to live our lives as government hand-me-down, needy people. That's not who we are. The older kids always have summer jobs. Elizabeth has been blessed to work year-round in the children's ministry at the church on the weekends. Being able to earn their own money has been a wonderful tool for teaching our kids responsibility. Rearing all of them to know that money doesn't grow on trees will only help them to work hard and succeed.

We set up bank accounts for the kids so that they will learn how to budget their money. We've taught them that when they are working, they will tithe. They know the reason we tithe is because God says that there is a commanded blessing to those who tithe. When they give God 10 percent of what He has given them, God Himself will rebuke the devourer for them, and they will be blessed (Mal. 3:8–10). Sion and I were determined to train all of our children in this biblical principle, just as the Lord had trained us over the years.

With a doctorate degree in pharmacy, Sion had an amazing potential for earning income. As a young married couple we understood the sacrifice we would be making when we stepped out into full-time ministry. There were times during those early days when the idea of going back to the financial security offered in the marketplace was appealing. But each time we experienced uncertainty, God granted us the peace to allow Him to walk us safely through each transition. He was always faithful to open just the right doors for us. As a result of our trusting Him, we had the peace that comes from knowing we were right where God wanted us, doing exactly what He wanted us to do.

As the executive worship pastor at Gateway Church, Sion had a good salary and great insurance coverage. I also got paid for the hours I worked at the church. But with eight children, we encountered many expenses that our basic income just couldn't cover. Even with the benefits the children received from Social Security and our careful budgeting, we knew that extracurricular activities were beyond our financial reach.

Sion and I were keenly aware of the importance of each child being involved in something at school. We had done the research and knew that kids make better grades and are inclined to do their best if they are actively involved in things within the community or within the school. Whether it's a club, a music group, or sports, we wanted each child involved in something that would help them develop their own unique gifts and abilities.

Out of their mutual love for their eight grandchildren, my parents set aside any personal differences to work together toward meeting their needs. Our family no doubt had suffered several great tragedies over the years. But by the grace of God, we were able to put down our offenses and the pain of the past to ensure that the next generation of our family grew up to be productive citizens who would fulfill the call of God on their individual lives. And it takes money to ensure that this happens.

Developing a budget required that Sion and I fully disclose both our income and monthly expenses to my parents. They knew exactly how much our income was and what Social Security would cover, as well as the cost of the extra activities for each child. Even today we could not fully provide everything that we believe God wants our children to have without the help of my parents. They have given of their time and treasure to ensure these children succeed. What a great love they have shown in laying down their lives. Jesus said, "If anyone would come after me, he must deny himself and take up his cross and follow me" (Mark 8:34).

No matter how difficult life becomes, we can develop a love relationship with God and choose the path to *follow Him*.

Chapter 8

THANK HIM

I COULDN'T BE MORE proud of my brother's children. They have gone from being victims of unspeakable tragedy to vibrant and victorious young people with a bright and meaningful future.

This experience has taught me to be still and wait on God.

The Bible says, "Those who wait for the LORD will gain new strength; they will mount up with wings like eagles, they will run and not get tired, they will walk and not become weary" (Isa. 40:31, NAS). We are living in perilous times. The enemy's plan is for us to lose hope and to believe God doesn't care or won't change our present circumstances. But if God is for us, then who can be against us? God does care about our circumstances, but He's more interested in the eternal perspective of changing us from the inside out, knowing everything else in life will someday fade away. Isaiah reminds us to wait and to place our hope in God. When we wait for the Lord, He promises three things will happen.

First, we will mount up with wings like eagles. In other words, we will fly over some things that we might have had to walk through if we hadn't waited for the Lord. This scripture is talking about abiding *in* Him instead of *with* Him. Let me ask you this: if you were asked to cross a large body of water, would you rather be *in* a boat or *with* a boat? Don't you agree it is safer and more time efficient to be in a boat than with a boat?

Second, when we wait on the Lord, He promises that we will run and not grow weary. No one likes to strive after the wind. It's futile and exhausting. We were all created for a purpose, and life is much easier when we are doing what we were created to do. What were we created to do? We were created to worship Him with our lives. If we love Him, we will passionately pursue Him. True passion, separated from our own ambitions, is surrendering our lives daily to Him and doing what He wants us to do.

Third, He says we will walk and not faint. When we wait on the Lord and place our hope in Him, we will never grow weary of doing good. We all need to gain new strength for the days ahead, so let's learn how to wait for the Lord and place our hope in the One who knows the beginning and the end. He is worthy of our praise and thanksgiving.

My husband, Sion, deserves the greatest applause. How many men would like to take on the responsibility of raising five more children than they already had? Not many, if any. It has been an overwhelming day-in, day-out task of monumental sacrifices for Sion, and I consider myself the most blessed woman in the world to have him as my husband. There is not a person on this planet who can make me laugh louder or cry harder than Sion Augustus Alford IV. His dad says we are a "match made in heaven." But as our pastor says, "Thunder and lightning are both in heaven." Still, I believe when God made Sion, He was thinking of me. There were similar interests that drew us together, but we have extreme differences that cause us to be a washbasin, as the Moabites were to the Israelites. (See Psalm 60:8.) Through the continual laundry cycles of life, we are learning how to love and honor one another above ourselves. After twenty years of marriage, I would do it all over again. As Bonnie Hunt, the mother in the movie *Cheaper by the Dozen*, said about her husband, Steve Martin, "He's still got it!"

As for my own children, kudos definitely go to my daughter, Brooke, who went from being the only girl in the house to being one of five girls. That was a huge challenge for her as she was entering her teenage years. Brooke and I have very different natural temperaments. As mothers and daughters often do, we had some struggles in coming together and appreciating each other. I think the challenge we faced as a family helped Brooke and me to work through some of our problem areas and taught us to really appreciate each other. There were also many things that she hadn't experienced by being an only daughter. It was amazing to watch her personal growth process as she learned to interact with her four new sisters.

My oldest son, Si, had to accept the fact that he was no longer the oldest child in the house. This was a fact that Elizabeth was all too happy to point out. Sion and I were proud of the way our son came to grips with the matter, saying, "It's OK; I am who I am." He was very secure in himself. He knew that life was going to be different, but he was able to see that it would be different with a better purpose. More things were going to happen as a result of his being able to reach out to his cousins as siblings. He realized that he could have more impact on other people's lives by allowing God to have His way in his own life. He saw the experience as a good thing, and, as always, he embraced the change of season and arose as a leader. He has received many outstanding awards both academically and among peers and teachers. As his parents, we are blessed. He is a light and witness wherever he goes and will continue to do great things because he follows hard after the Lord.

Austin, our youngest son, was once the baby of the family, but overnight he became a big brother. When Caroline first moved in, she wouldn't leave my side. No matter what I was doing, she would wait for me, even when I was going to the bathroom. She hugged me all of the time and wanted to call me Mom, but Austin wouldn't agree to that name. So we came up with "Nene" (pronounced nee'·nee) since she hugged my knees all day. Eventually all of my brother's children started calling me "Nene" and Sion "Pops" since we were more than guardians; we were loving parents. This was a difficult process for Austin, but he has matured into a very well-rounded, compassionate, and strong young man. He is very responsible and has been a huge encouragement to David and Emily that hard work pays off.

From the time the kids started their first year of school together in the new school district, they referred to each other as sisters and brothers. Over time they shared their story with those who became their close friends. Today some of their friends know they are cousins, but most people look at them as brothers and sisters.

When my brother's children came to live with us, I wanted to make sure that they didn't feel any different from any other child in school. While we always honored the memory of their mother and father, we wanted them to feel that they were as loved and cared for as anyone else in their schools. As the eldest, it was more of a struggle for Elizabeth to get to the place where she actually felt she was safe and protected.

Several of the children dreaded the first day of school. They feared what others would think of them if they knew the children had guardians, not parents. To those who were nervous, I said, "My middle name, Schwartz, happens to be your last name, so no one will ask you any questions." Not wanting to draw any attention to himself, David addressed me as his mom from day one at school—and that I was. When children in the hallway would say, "Hey, Mrs. Schwartz," or "That's David's mom," I would smile and wave.

Caroline struggled with what to do but tried to not make it as obvious; that is, until one day after school when she got in the car and asked, "Nene, am I an orphan?"

"No!" I said. "Why are you asking me that?"

"Today, in front of everyone in my class, this boy told me I was an orphan because I didn't have any parents."

"Well, what did you say?" I asked.

She said, "I do too."

Then I said, "That's exactly right. You *do* have a mom and dad who love you very much."

I assured Caroline that she had nothing to be embarrassed about and that she was loved. I'm not sure what her calling is, but she'll go toe to toe with anyone. Now, all of that boldness is harnessed to follow Him. She has to make members of the dark side shake in their boots. She is an amazing Jedi in training for the kingdom of

God and is dearly loved by Him. I know this for sure, since the Bible says God is a father to the fatherless (see Psalm 68:5), and Psalm 10:14 says, "But you, O God, do see trouble and grief; you consider it to take it in hand. The victim commits himself to you; you are the helper of the fatherless."

While we were still going through the tumultuous process of confirming guardianship, we told the children that they were all worth fighting for. I remember saying to them, "We know that God has a plan and a purpose for you. I cannot tell you that the things that happened to you were God's will, because God is not a mean and cruel God. But I can say that He does work out all things for good for those who love Him and who are called according to His purpose. And each and every one of you *is* called according to His purpose.

"You each have a destiny. I can see that where you were, you were not going to be able to reach your full potential. You would not have been able to do all that God wants you to do. So here in this place, you have a place of safety. You have a church where you can go and get help. You have an aunt and uncle who love you and who want to pour into your life. We want to see you healed, and then at the proper time, we want to release you to go and do what God has called you to do."

This is my prayer for all my children:

> Do not let your hearts be troubled (distressed, agitated). You *believe* in and *adhere* to and *trust*

> in and *rely* on God; believe in and adhere to and trust in and rely also on Me.
>
> —John 14:1, amp, emphasis added

- **Believe:** "I wait for the Lord, my soul waits, and in his word I put my hope" (Ps. 130:5).
- **Adhere:** "From the ends of the earth I call to you, I call as my heart grows faint; lead me to the rock that is higher than I" (Ps. 61:2).
- **Trust:** "I will say of the Lord, 'He is my refuge and my fortress, my God, in whom I trust'" (Ps. 91:2).
- **Rely:** "My salvation and my honor depend on God; he is my mighty rock, my refuge. Trust in him at all times, O people; pour out your hearts to him, for God is our refuge" (Ps. 62:7–8).

Today all of the children, including Elizabeth, are secure enough in our love that they refer to Sion and me as their parents. We thank God every day that they feel safe enough to do so. We are also thankful for the many men and women whom God has placed around us to offer support and guidance as we've made this journey together as a family. One person who made a significant impact on our lives is Pastor Tom Lane at Gateway Church.

It was Pastor Tom who first shared with us the idea of making a family covenant. Pastor Tom and his wife have four children who are now grown with families of their own. He told us that while the kids were still young and at home, they had come up with a set of standards and guidelines about how they wanted to treat each other as a family and what was expected as they were with their friends outside the home.

Although Sion and I had set verbal guidelines and rules for some things, we had never written anything down on paper so that our children could visually see what we were asking them and why. We didn't want to isolate our children from the world. Rather, we wanted to teach them how to be a light in the world as Kari Jobe's 2012 CD declares, "We are the light of the world." It was Jesus Himself who said, "You are the light of the world. A city on a hill cannot be hidden. Neither do people light a lamp and put it under a bowl. Instead they put it on its stand, and it gives light to everyone in the house. In the same way, let your light shine before men, that they may see your good deeds and praise your Father in heaven" (Matt. 5:14–16).

As amazing and easy as technology has made our lives, there is a world of darkness our children are exposed to on a daily basis. I'm thankful Sion is knowledgeable about upgrading software and dealing with hard-drive issues. This can be an irritating and time-consuming process, but we have all watched him in total admiration as he makes checklists and troubleshoots programming errors, safeguarding our computers from potential sites or games that are not appropriate or could harm the children.

If it wasn't for his determination and quest for the latest super-duper, high-tech, flux capacitor and rocket-launching computer system, we would still be using ledgers and address books and have no clue as to what our children are exposed to on a daily basis. His attitude and diligence in maintaining our earthly possessions for everyday life have been a blessing and a safeguard to the character-building process of Christ being formed in our lives. We have a covenant that holds us accountable for our computers and cell phones so that we live in the light as He is in the light. We love our daddy!

Also within this family covenant, Pastor Tom outlined how they were going to deal with various situations. The idea was to have a road map to follow as issues presented themselves. "Whenever anything would come up, we'd have our covenant to refer to," he said. "If any of the children made a bad decision, we could point to the document and show them they had broken the covenant. The family covenant was something we could always refer back to. It was a contract, and there would be consequences for breaking the rules."

Sion and I knew that creating a covenant in which every person would have input was just what our family needed. We called everyone together around our special "come to Jesus" table and explained what we were about to do: Sion and I would write the initial draft, which would include scriptures to back up the general principles that would be laid out. Then the children would look it over and add any vital components that we may have overlooked.

We didn't want to create a document that felt like it was a set of rules set forth just because we were the parents and what we said was so. Remember, we all hated it when our parents answered our question by saying, "Because I said so!" We wanted a living covenant that expressed our beliefs and who we were as a family. We wanted a format in which truths would be simple enough for even the youngest members to understand.

Once we had the document exactly the way we wanted it, we all came together around the table and took turns signing it. I am sharing our family's covenant in this book so that other families might use it as inspiration for setting forth their own guiding principles.

The Alford/Schwartz Family Covenant

First and foremost, we commit as a family to uphold the greatest desire of the Lord: "Love the Lord your God with all your heart and with all your soul and with all your mind and with all your strength. The second is this: 'Love your neighbor as yourself.' There is no commandment greater than these" (Mark 12:30–31).

As a family, joined together by God's will and plan, we covenant with one another to live by and accomplish the following three purposes in our lives:

1. Our Purpose Is to Love

As mentioned in the verse above, it is our purpose to love God with all of our hearts, souls, minds, and strength and to love each other as we love ourselves. We will run every thought, motive, and action through the filter of the following verse: "Love is patient and kind. Love is not jealous or boastful or proud or rude. It does not demand its own way. It is not irritable, and it keeps no record of being wronged. It does not rejoice about injustice but rejoices whenever the truth wins out. Love never gives up, never loses faith, is always hopeful, and endures through every circumstance" (1 Cor. 13:4–7, NLT).

2. Our Purpose Is to Lead

It is our purpose to influence as many people as we can for God and His kingdom. It is our desire to represent God through our conduct in our personal life and through our conduct in our work/community/school life. We will live by the Spirit of God and conduct our life consistent with biblical principles so that we honor God in all that we do. We will satisfy the appetites of our lives in ways that are approved by God. "Because we have these promises, dear friends, let us cleanse ourselves from everything that can defile our body or spirit. And let us work toward complete holiness because we fear God" (2 Cor. 7:1, NLT).

3. Our Purpose Is to Live

It is our desire to live in the presence of God with the realization that He is omnipresent and apart from Him there is no life. It is our passion to walk and live in the perfect and complete will of God, believing that the life God has for us is fun, adventurous, and exciting, but can also be challenging and difficult at times. Our purpose is to fulfill His will for our lives as we walk in a worship relationship with Him. "Therefore, I urge you, brothers, in view of God's mercy, to offer your bodies as living sacrifices, holy and pleasing to God—this is your spiritual act of worship. Do not conform any longer to the pattern of this world, but be transformed by the renewing of your mind. Then you will be able to test and approve what God's will is—his good, pleasing and perfect will" (Rom. 12:1–2).

We commit to this covenant on this twentieth day of March, 2011, and as a family, we pray the following for our lives: "And I pray that you, being rooted and established in love, may have power, together with all the saints, to grasp how wide and long and high and deep is the love of Christ, and to know this love that surpasses knowledge—that you may be filled to the measure of all the fullness of God. Now to him who is able to do immeasurably more than all we ask or imagine, according to his power that is at work within us, to him be glory in the church and in Christ Jesus throughout all generations, for ever and ever! Amen" (Eph. 3:17–21).

______________________	______________________
Sion Alford	Shannon Alford
______________________	______________________
Elizabeth Schwartz	Si Alford
______________________	______________________
Mary Catherine Schwartz	Brooke Alford
______________________	______________________
Emily Schwartz	Austin Alford
______________________	______________________
David Schwartz	Caroline Schwartz

Since creating our family covenant in 2011, we have had the opportunity to go back to it many times and use it as a guiding light in various situations. Once we had firmly established a covenant foundation of love in our family, we were then able to build other principles into our lives.

We had talked to the children early on about the power that our words carry. That power can be either good or bad. The Book of Proverbs refers to words as the fruit of our lips, saying, "From the fruit of their lips people enjoy good things, but the unfaithful have an appetite for violence" (Prov. 13:2).

Unfaithful people are people who are not full of faith. Rather, they allow fear to dictate their actions. Our Maltese dog (I know, he isn't a person, but we treat him like the baby of the family) responds in fear every day, but we still love him. If something startles him, he barks violently until I pick him up and assure him there is no danger. Then he returns to being a little lamb. The children will tease him and say, "Dallas, you are so brave," because now he is in Mommy's arms and is full of faith that I will protect him. Thank God, He is our defender.

When David moved to Texas, he couldn't ride a bike without experiencing frustration and outbursts of anger that would arise when he fell or was teased by the other children. He was eight years old and still had a bike with training wheels. It was our mission to build his confidence and faith in the fact that he could ride a bike just like Caroline, Austin, and Emily. For weeks Sion worked with David, but every time he failed, it took my holding him in order to get him to calm down and stop crying. Then Sion would place the training wheels back on the bike. Oftentimes David screamed at the others for teasing him while they rode their bikes with no hands. Then one day I told him, "David, today is your big day. Pops (Sion's guardian name) is taking the training wheels off your bike." After one more big push and having Sion run beside him to ensure he wouldn't fall, David finally mastered the art and balance of riding a bike. All the children and some neighbors cheered, "Go, David!" Others had a few tears of joy, knowing he had almost given up hope of ever accomplishing this feat. We watched a once fearful, violent, raging child turn into a faith-filled, happy boy. Although it took us over a year to help David overcome his fears and believe he could be who God had called him to be, we all watched God's Word change a soul. Our words have power.

Speaking of power, another familiar scripture comes to mind: "The tongue has the power of life and death, and those who live it will eat its fruit" (Prov. 18:21).

Using this scripture as our basis of truth, we explained to the children that we were not going to allow anyone to plant any fruit that they didn't want to have to eat. In other words, there would be no tolerance of any verbal communication that tore down another family member. We painted a picture of our words being like seeds planted in a garden. "When it comes harvest time and we don't like what we have to reap, we can't blame someone else, and we can't blame God," I said. "We're the ones who planted the seed, and we are therefore responsible for what is grown. Our family covenant will not tolerate anything less than the law of love upon our tongues."

Sion and I have seen tremendous growth in ourselves and in the children since we established our family covenant. I know our children are particularly blessed to have a dad who makes spending a lot of good quality time with them a priority in his life. I think what has made another difference for all of the children is there's a good healthy balance of daily activities. We know that when it's time to work, we do what is expected and get our work done. But when it's time to play, we have a fun time. They know Sion and I will set time aside daily and will spend time with them. That's priceless. Money can't buy that. Only God can give the peace and assurance to trust in the vision and purpose He has given us for raising our children while taking time to enjoy the journey.

Sion and I see our role as parents as a vital one. We have made the commitment to pour ourselves into our children, the future mothers and fathers of the next generation. We are teaching them that they will have to make some sacrifices for their families. We want them to understand that it takes an investment of time and emotion to build a well-rounded family with God at its center.

As a result of our own efforts, we have been blessed to watch our children grow in character. They are learning how to identify and develop their God given talents and abilities as they seek God's will for their lives. The Bible says that "sons are a heritage from the Lord, children a reward from him. Like arrows in the hands of a warrior are sons born in one's youth. Blessed is the man whose quiver is full of them" (Ps. 127:3–5).

To keep our children as arrows in our quiver and not thorns in our flesh, we saw the importance of sitting down with each one individually and helping them write out a vision for their lives so that we could help them accomplish their goals and pray over them for God's perfect will to be done. The Bible says, "Write the vision and make it plain on tablets, that he may run who reads it" (Hab. 2:2, NKJV). We also shared with them Proverbs 16:1–3, which says, "We can make our own plans, but the LORD gives the right answer. People may be pure in their own eyes, but the LORD examines their motives. Commit your actions to the LORD, and your plans will succeed" (NLT).

By sitting down and writing things out, we created a valuable, well-spent opportunity that would help them develop their talents and give them a vision for their future as opposed to just letting life happen. Everyone needs a vision so that they can see where they are and where they are going. Periodically throughout the year we revise and revisit our visions so that as we grow together, we are able to see God's will more clearly. Truly we are blessed, and we thank Him for His blessings.

> Therefore, I urge you, brothers, in view of God's mercy, to offer your bodies as living sacrifices, holy and pleasing to God—this is your spiritual act of worship. Do not conform any longer to the pattern of this world, but be transformed by the renewing of your mind. Then you will be able to test and approve what God's will is—his good, pleasing and perfect will.
>
> —ROMANS 12:1–2

Every day we are living worship. We've all read the notice in the church bulletin or on the sign out front that says "Worship Service" and then gives the time. We've been programmed to believe that worship is something we do at church. As a teenager, I was taught that the way to tell if you were really worshipping God was if you got goose bumps during the slow songs and Sister Susie twirled down the aisles with her tambourine and streamers.

My husband, Sion, has taught for many years that although the words *praise* and *worship* are used interchangeably in our Christian culture, they have very different biblical meanings. Praise is a declarative word. Anybody can praise God, even those who are not believers. For instance, when someone says, "Wow, what a beautiful sunset," that's praising God for what He's done.

Worship, on the other hand, is declaring who God is. It's expressing His attributes. God is love, joy, peace, patience, kindness, goodness, faithfulness, and so much more. As we allow His attributes to bear fruit in our own lives on a daily basis, our living worship allows others to see who God really is.

For over twenty years my husband and I have been worship leaders and songwriters. We have taught thousands of others how to be lead worshippers. But how many know true worship is not what you go and do but what you live? True worship begins when self is placed on the altar daily. That means seven days a week and twenty-four hours a day you offer yourself as a living sacrifice to God. The only way to live *in* God's will is to give Him your life on a daily basis. Otherwise you are merely living *with* God's will.

Overnight our living worship took our family from aunts and uncles to moms and dads, from cousins to siblings, and from five people in a house to ten people living together. God's will led our worship to become a sacrifice. We all want God's promises (His healing, provision, protection), but to walk in His will requires the daily sacrifice of our own will. When we live in God's will, we learn to be thankful for Him and for His promises. We know it is not we who are accomplishing God's will through our lives, but it is Christ who lives on the inside.

> God makes no promise that life will be fair
> But He does promise He will take you through
> every storm because He does care.
> If you are struggling with past hurts and pain,
> Lay down your life and you will gain.
> Far greater than your eyes can fathom
> The glorious hope His love has ransomed.
> Don't let yourself be deceived,
> You serve a master every day in word and deed.
> So willfully give your life up for His
> And receive the reward of being living worship
> for Him.

The psalmist wrote, "I will bless the Lord at all times; His praise shall continually be in my mouth. My soul shall make its boast in the Lord; the humble shall hear of it and be glad. Oh, magnify the Lord with me, and let us exalt His name together" (Ps. 34:1–3, NKJV).

Let's pray:

> *Lord, let us realize everything we do on a daily basis is worship and our living worship allows Your will to be done in our lives. We surrender our lives and we choose to bless You at all times. Amen!*

He loves it when we *thank Him.*

—Shannon Alford

CONCLUSION

Essays From the Children

When I share with others that my husband and I are raising eight children as a result of what happened to our family, immediately people want to pat us on the back and tell us what saints we are. In reality, we know we are sinners saved by grace, and we are thankful for the trials we have faced that have brought us to love God and others with all our heart, soul, mind, and strength.

Sion and I have come to appreciate the true beauty of the transformation process that has made it possible for us to fulfill God's call as we yield our lives to Him. As I shared in chapter 1, when I asked Sion if he would have married me had he known we would be raising eight children, he immediately answered no. Truth be told, if we had both known in those early years what lay before us, we would have tried to bypass that part of our journey together. Why? Because we weren't yet prepared to do what God was calling us to do. But we know that He who begins a good work is always faithful to complete it.

Coming together as one family has been a challenging experience for all of us. But it has given us a deeper love for God, who has been faithful to work all things for our good.

I asked the children to write an essay about their experience in hopes that what they share will be helpful to someone else who is dealing with life's struggles and disappointments. I trust you will be blessed by the words they share as they pour out their hearts.

Elizabeth Schwartz

It all started with June 14, 2006, a day that changed my life forever. My dad, Michael Scott Schwartz, passed away due to lung cancer. He was, until that day, my best friend. I told him everything, did everything with him, and talked to him more than any other person on earth. He was the best dad I could ever ask for. He always had my back. But after that day I've never been the same.

Soon after that I started high school, and in May of 2009, my mother, Stacey Moody Schwartz, passed away from a sudden heart attack. I could never tell you which death was harder to endure, but I can tell you that from each of these life-changing events, different character traits have been built and strengthened, and still continue to be strengthened, in me.

The days that followed May 14, 2009, were a blur. Things happened so fast. Well, of course, there were five kids to take care of! My four siblings and I were now orphans, no parents. That's how everyone would tease us anyways.

In July of 2009, we were taken in by my aunt and uncle that we now call Nene and Pops. At first I didn't want to be in Texas. I had left the place where I had grown up, all my friends were there, and the majority of my family was living in Florida. I came here having to start all over. I had to make new friends, start at a new school, and live with a new family. I was so scared to come here because, for me, making friends was a hard task. But as always, God to the rescue!

Brittany was the first girl I met at Byron Nelson High School. My aunt and her mom were on the worship team together at Gateway Church, and they introduced us to each other at school. We were both there for the color guard class. She has been my best friend ever since. And I thank God for her and the other people that He has placed in my life.

As God has softened my heart along the way to see that He works everything for the good of those who love Him and who are called according to His purpose, I saw everything good that was happening inside my heart and in the hearts of my siblings. I now see that this place is a good place for me. Troubles come every day with new challenges and new tasks to take on. Through my life I have learned that God's way is the best. Yes, I know the tunnel may be dark, but there is always light at the end. God is continuing to work in my heart and teach me things that make me more like Him. The most important thing that I could tell someone who goes through hard times is this: everything happens for a reason, but with love, faith, and God, you will be unstoppable.

Love the good times, have faith through the bad times, and trust God through it all.

Si Alford

When I heard that my five cousins were going to come live with us, at first I thought that my parents were just tossing around suggestions at the dinner table. I never dreamed it was a reality they were seriously considering.

It did not become apparent that my cousins were actually heading here from Florida until my parents purchased a fifteen-passenger van.

I was extremely glad to have familiar faces around. Middle school was a very troubling time for me as a kid because I could not find good Christian friends. I never found my place or a group I could hang with, and I struggled through a lot during that time. I think personally that I accepted the change quickly and the larger family with open arms because I really wanted to move where I could be a part of a great youth group and find great Christian friends.

I have learned so much from having more brothers and sisters come into my life. It has taught me to love and care for other people and to consider that everyone has a story to tell and struggles in life. I don't ever judge a book by its cover because although the pages may be tattered and the cover may not look as nice, it is what is on the inside that counts. I want to give God glory throughout my life through the gifts and talents that He has given me. Even if my pages look "tattered," God still has a plan and calls it beautiful when I surrender my life to Him.

I would be lying if I didn't say that there are some mornings when I wake up and ask God, "Where did they come from, and how did they get here?" Questions like these make me realize that God has really made the situation turn out for the better and made us all better people. There are drawbacks, but the limitations are tiny compared to the blessing of a large family.

I thank God every day for His goodness throughout these years and never regret one day! God has taught me a lot through this situation, and I only look forward to what God is going to do through us in the future!

Mary Catherine Schwartz

May 14, 2009. I thought it was going to be like any other day until I walked downstairs into my mom's room. I thought it was odd that her music wasn't playing throughout the house like it was every morning. I usually went down there every morning to spend time with my mom and watch her do her makeup. But this Thursday morning was different, very different.

I walked into her room to find her lying on her bed gripping her chest. I didn't know what to do; I was in utter shock. I went over by her and called "Mom" a few times to see if she was just sleeping, but when she didn't respond, I knew that my life would be very different from that day on.

I ran up the stairs calling to my sister Elizabeth for her help. I couldn't make out any words, so all I could say was "Mom!" She knew exactly what I meant because she knew our mom had a heart problem. She told our cousin Matt to call 911 and tell them that our mom wasn't responding. We called everyone we thought should be the first to know.

The next few weeks were a blur. My life was changed. The thoughts that went through my mind were, "Where are we going to live? Who are we going to live with? How am I supposed to live without my mom, my best friend?"

My four siblings and I stayed at my house with different family members until we all got done with school. While we were in school, my family was trying to figure out who would stay with whom and where. It was a big hassle and a burden for them to have to struggle to figure it out. After the court date, my brother and sisters and I ended up in Texas. I would have never imagined myself living there. We were going to live with my aunt and uncle and their three kids.

When I first moved to Texas, I was in deep depression, but I never told anyone. It was very hard for me not to see any of my old friends and family that I had grown up with my whole life. It was a whole different world. I was going into high school with no friends and no mom or dad that I could talk to about it or have them counsel me through it and say it was going to be OK. I was angry and upset at what had happened in my life. I thought everyone looked at me differently because I didn't have parents. I thought I was labeled as "the orphan." When people would try to help me with things, I shut them out. I didn't want anyone to be close to me because I couldn't trust anyone.

Moving to Texas was a complete shock to what I was used to because my aunt and uncle had very different rules and guidelines to follow. I was in shock how they lived and everything they believed. I almost felt childish having to learn right from wrong all over again. I was upset and didn't want to move here, but I never told anyone how I was feeling. Going into high school not knowing or trusting anyone, you tend to feel lonely. Walking into class without recognizing a single face or voice is not a comforting feeling. I felt so left out and lonely because no one knew me or even tried to make friends with me, but then again I shut everyone out.

I remember walking into my theater class and clicking with this girl named Kate. She was new to Texas, and she didn't know anyone either. We became the best of friends. I am so thankful that I have her today because I wouldn't be able to make it through high school without her. She was the first person I could trust after I lost my mom and I moved here. She is still today the one person who knows everything about me and what I'm going through (other than my family).

No one knew about my tragic past, and I didn't tell anyone. I tried to keep it a secret as much as I could because I didn't want to be labeled as a freak or an orphan because I didn't have parents and I lived with my aunt and uncle. I was ashamed of my life, and that was a stronghold I needed to break. I became distant from God, and that's who I needed to help me with the pain and hurt from my mother's death and moving away from my hometown, moving away from the people I was closest with and who I trusted with everything.

After I sought out the Lord and asked Him to help me and guide me through life, I got over being embarrassed and ashamed of my life. Not having anyone I could trust with the secrets of my life was a hard thing to live with. I opened up to many more people and became a better person altogether. When I found out they had a swim team at school, I joined the team without hesitation. I didn't know anyone on the team, and once again I felt left out. I had to prove myself to my coaches and my new swim mates. I was very quiet, and I didn't open up to my team until I was a sophomore. I just swam when I was told, and I never talked. I was really shy with everyone except my best friend, Kate.

I now have many friends, and I trust people more. I am thankful for what God has blessed me with: a great family, friends, and a swim team. I have also learned that God doesn't give us more than we can handle, so I can't wait to see what He has in store for me. I am closer to my family, and I actually love Texas! It is such a great state to live in, and it has so many open doors and opportunities for me to go forward in my swimming.

Brooke Alford

When we first found out my cousins would be living with us, I was very excited because we only saw them once or twice a year. Being the only girl, I was looking forward to having sisters both younger and older. Sharing my parents at first was almost unnoticeable, but after a while it got old and kind of annoying. I had to learn to share and make the most of the opportunities I did have with my parents. It isn't easy, but it has made me love my mom and dad more.

When we found out we were moving, I was a little nervous about leaving my friends and having to start over and make new friends. I now love living in Trophy Club because the drive to church is only ten minutes compared to an hour. It has also allowed me to be a part of the youth group and leadership in mission trips over the years, which has changed my attitude about how blessed I am. I love my new friends and know I'm blessed to have such a great technologically advanced school.

Still, my greatest challenge has been sharing. I used to be the only girl, so I didn't have to share anything, but now it's the opposite. There are times I miss all the attention and privacy, but I have learned to do unto others as you would want them to do unto you. The good thing is, I'm never bored and there is always someone to talk to. I'm learning how to cope with not getting everything I want, even though receiving gifts is my love language.

I am in the medical academy at school, and my future plans are to be a pediatric or neonatal nurse. I love babysitting in my neighborhood, and it brings me joy to help moms with their small children.

If I could give anyone advice about walking through difficult times, it would be keep your head up, read your Bible, and don't let Satan try and bring you down or break you apart.

Emily Schwartz

When my dad passed away, it was really shocking. I was very sad because he was funny and made us all laugh. It made me a stronger person and able to get through things, but I still was very sad. Then when my mom passed away, I couldn't believe that both my parents were gone. It was unbearable.

I don't think my relationship was as strong with my mom as I wanted it to be. I felt like she was never satisfied with me and I was never good enough. I felt like I had to prove myself to her instead of feeling loved for who I was. I know she loved me, but I feel like she didn't always show it. I wanted to be appreciated, but no one really thanked me for anything I did. I never dreamed the last time I would see her would be when I was climbing on a bus to go to St. Augustine on a field trip for a week with my fifth-grade elementary class. I remember her waving and giving me the "I love you" sign as we drove off.

I didn't want to leave Florida. No one really told me what was going on, so after Mom died, I was just hopping all around friends' and family's houses and doing what I was told to do. I was very sad and worried what was going to happen next.

I was not happy when I found out I was leaving my family and all my friends. I only saw my cousins in Texas twice a year, so I didn't think they would like me living with them. I didn't want to go and thought my aunt and uncle were taking me away forever. At first I thought Brooke was rude, but now we are both trying out for cheerleading together. I thought Austin didn't want us here because he didn't want us touching his things, but now we play together and have fun. Now I'm glad we are here in Texas because I got saved and it has drawn me closer to the Lord. I like singing on the children's worship team, and I hope someday to sing in big church. I have a lot of good friends, and I still stay in contact by phone with my best friend, Kate, in Florida.

I like being in a big family and having all the different personalities come together under one roof. It's always a party. I love when people ask me how many siblings I have and I say I am one of eight. They always flip out, and I think it's great!

I will be a freshman next year, and I recently got accepted into the culinary school. I want to be a chef when I grow up.

My greatest challenge was learning how to be responsible with my grades. My aunt and uncle promised me a phone this past Christmas if I kept up with my grades. This has been a new concept for me to learn, but I'm glad to learn how to be more responsible, and I now have a phone.

If I could share advice with someone who has lost a parent or parents, I would tell them to pray to God and

He will always be a dad that will never leave their side. When I got saved, I felt a million pounds come off me. I knew that God was the person I could go to if I didn't have a good day, and I could tell Him all about how I was feeling. I think about how I lost my mom and dad, and it has made me a strong person in my heart. I can go through anything that goes on in my life because of God.

Austin Alford

When I first realized that my cousins were going to live with us, I was honestly quite happy because David was like a brother to me every time I went to Florida to visit. But the only bad thing about it was that I wasn't the baby anymore. I was a big brother to Caroline and David, not a little brother to Si and Brooke. I didn't like it very much when they first came because Caroline got to be the baby and get all the cool stuff, and I didn't get to spend a lot of time with my parents alone. But I got used to it over time.

I was a little nervous about moving to Trophy Club and making new friends. I shared with my fifth-grade teacher about all the changes that had happened to my family, and so she helped me adjust to my new environment. David and I became like brothers, and we talked and helped each other with problems and concerns.

Well, the biggest problem I had to overcome was that I was pretty selfish because I didn't really have to share with anybody when it was just Si and Brooke. So when my cousins came, I had to learn how to share with others.

What I missed the most about the past was that I was the baby and pretty much got a lot of awesome and cool things from my parents. Although the bigger the family, the more fun you have during nights that we go out to eat and do fun things together as a big happy family. I still love it when one of my parents can take me out to eat at a restaurant and we can talk about things on our heart.

So far, my plans and goals are to be on the main worship team at church so that I can grow more experienced playing guitar and leading the music. Then I would create a band with my friends so that we can travel around the globe and play for Jesus Christ. If I could share with someone that was going to move in with their cousins or be placed in another home, I would tell the person to get out of a habit of being selfish and learn how to play with your toys with others because you're going to need to know how to share.

David Schwartz

When I found out my dad had passed away, I was speechless because he had told me the day before that when he died, I would be the man of the house. I didn't expect this at five years old. I was angry and afraid of what would happen to me and my sisters.

Before my dad passed away, I remember my mom had to go to the store, so she left my dad and all of us at the house. He was very sick and in a lot of pain. My little sister, Caroline, climbed up on a bookshelf, and it fell on top of her. I thought she was going to die. My dad picked up the shelf off her and she was OK, but we were all scared she was going to be hurt for life.

I was a very loud and rowdy boy before my dad passed away. It made me quiet and unwilling to talk at all, especially to strangers. I would stay up late watching TV until

I would be too tired to stay awake. But I would still wake up early to check on my sisters because I was afraid of losing them. My sisters became very valuable to me.

After my dad passed away, I wasn't at the house very often. After school I would go to a friend's house depending on what day it was. The day before my mom passed away, I remember riding with a friend, coming home from school, and being dropped off at my house. My mom was home with Caroline. She had picked Caroline up from preschool. My mom was resting on the couch and Caroline was playing with toys on the floor. I passed my mom and said hey and went upstairs to play.

That night she told us she wasn't feeling good and sent Elizabeth to make sure we brushed our teeth and went to bed. The next morning I heard crying and running up and down the stairs. I woke up, and Elizabeth, my oldest sister, told me that mom had passed away. She said she felt bad for not checking on her and making sure she'd taken her blood pressure medicine before she went to bed. Elizabeth was crying so hard that when she called 911, she gave the phone to my cousin Matthew (who had spent the night with us) so that he could talk to the police.

Now my mom had passed away and there was no one to take care of us. I was so afraid and didn't know where I would live. For weeks I switched back and forth between houses and environments. I tried to adapt to each environment, but I never felt rested. I felt like any minute a timer would go off and then I would move again. After I moved to Texas, I took almost a year before I felt settled and I liked my new environment. I was upset because I had to move. I was taken away from everything that was familiar. I liked warm, damp weather, and everything in Texas was dry.

When I moved to Texas, I was glad that Austin liked me and introduced me to Legos and sports. I learned how to ride a bike, and it made me feel strong and confident about myself. I was glad to go to church on a regular basis, but it was new for me. When we moved to Texas, I was glad we were all together, but it was hard to adjust to having older brothers. Austin challenged me. It was hard learning how to get along and share as well. It was very strange going from parents to guardians. I wanted parents because it made me feel safe.

All of these situations affected the way I viewed life. One night at church I gave my heart to God. I didn't know Him for who He was, but now I know Christmas is Jesus's birthday, and before moving, I didn't treat it that way. There are three things that have affected my life the most: meeting Christ, riding my bike, and learning about responsibility. Having to do chores and stay up with my schoolwork was a huge challenge. I didn't like being bossed around by anyone. After being disciplined and being together, it made me more understanding.

When I moved to a new school, I wasn't very assertive because I didn't know anyone in my class. The teachers made me feel like I could make it even though I wasn't the strongest person in the class. My family helped me see myself as a smart person and not an orphan. I felt so loved when Nene and Pops received full guardianship of my sisters and me. I miss seeing my old friends, but I love that Nene cooks for me every day.

My future goals are to work in the government as a representative of Texas or Florida. I know tragedy when

I see it, and I easily show compassion and do something about it. I believe you can't represent the people unless you know the people. So my quest is to be friendly and interested in people. For example, I like meeting new students and making them feel welcome.

Caroline Schwartz

I was very sad when my dad and mom died because I didn't spend time with them. My mom worked, and I would go to my friend's house; then when I would come back home, she would be too tired to tuck me in at night. When I first heard we were moving from Florida to Texas, I was sad because I would miss my dogs, and I didn't know what was going to happen to me or where I was going to live. I wished my parents wouldn't have smoked so that this wouldn't have happened.

The first day of school, I was really scared. It made me feel uncomfortable when people would ask why my mom's nametag was different from mine. I would feel like I had to tell them the whole story, and it would make me feel so bad. I was sad and mad and sometimes angry with God. Then I realized He was trying to make life better for me. I am the most thankful for God saving me, leading me to be a part of this family, and that I have a dog. My greatest challenge was making new friends, but I decided Texas would be fine to grow up in, and I felt protected.

When I first moved here, I didn't really know my cousins, and I was nervous that I would be picked on the most because I was the youngest. Then I was happy to be here, but I had to learn new rules. I miss not having a lot of animals. I love when our family goes places and we spend time with each other. What means the most to me is when our family sits at the table together and plays games or eats.

My future goals are I want to move back to Florida and be an animal cop and save all the animals.

ABOUT THE AUTHOR

Shannon Alford serves on the worship team at Gateway Church in Southlake, Texas. Her husband, Sion Alford, is an executive worship pastor at the church. They both currently are a part of the weekend worship team and write songs for their worship CDs, which are released nationally.

Shannon and Sion are originally from Florida and released six albums prior to moving to Texas. One album, *Fresh Fire*, was released nationally and opened the doors for them to travel to many churches throughout the United States and internationally, teaching on praise and worship.

Shannon graduated from Florida State University with a bachelor of science degree in clothing, textiles, and merchandising. She also has a bachelor of theology degree from Christian Life School of Theology in Macon, Georgia.

Shannon and Sion have been married for twenty years and are blessed to have eight children, ages eight to eighteen. They reside in Dallas, Texas.

CONTACT THE AUTHOR

To get more information about the ministry of Shannon Alford and to view more ministry resources, please feel free to visit or connect with Shannon via the following social media avenues:

Website
www.247worshipministries.com

Facebook
8 Is Enough

Twitter
@shannonalford

Telephone
877.646.5640

DAD AND ME IN PNG
LIZZY GARDNER AINSWORTH

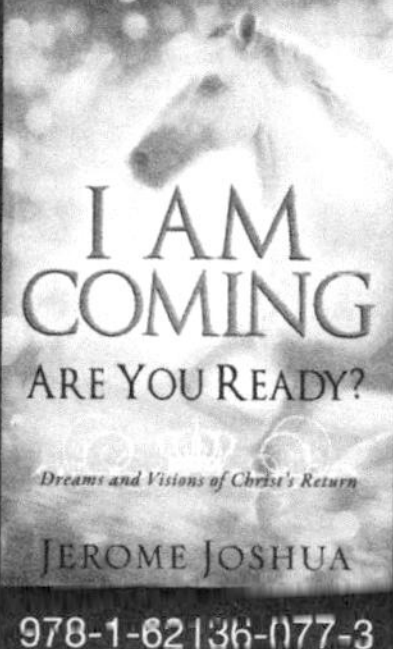
I AM COMING
ARE YOU READY?
Dreams and Visions of Christ's Return
JEROME JOSHUA

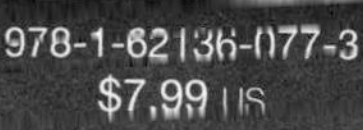

KICK ANXIETY
Let Go of Anxiety and Live With the Peace of God
ANNE LAIDLAW

MASON MICHAEL